Power of Your Love

Jesus: The Unexpected God

GEOFF BULLOCK

Strand Publishing
SYDNEY

Power of Your Love. Jesus: The Unexpected God
Copyright © 2000 Geoff Bullock

This book is copyright. Apart from any use as permitted under the *Copyright Act 1968*, no part may be reproduced by any process without prior written permission of the publisher.

First published 2000 by Strand Publishing

ISBN 187 682 5499

Distributed in Australia by:
Family Reading Publications
B100 Ring Road
Ballarat Victoria 3352
Phone: 03 5334 3244
Fax: 03 5334 3299
Email: enquiries@familyreading.com.au
Web: www.familyreading.com.au

All Scripture quotations are taken from *The Holy Bible, New King James Version*. Copyright © 1979, 1980, 1982 by Thomas Nelson, Inc. Used by permission. All rights reserved.

Edited by Owen Salter
Cover design by Joy Lankshear
Cover photo used by permission of Museo del Prado
Typesetting by Midland Typesetters, Maryborough, Victoria
Printed by Australian Print Group, Maryborough, Victoria

Contents

Acknowledgments		v
Introduction		1
1	Interpretations and Expectations	5
2	The Grace of His Coming	17
3	The Stage Is Set	27
4	Nazareth	39
5	Arise, Shine	52
6	Cana	62
7	Capernaum	75
8	Outcasts	93
9	John the Baptist	108
10	Peter	121
11	Rich, Young and Upwardly Mobile	141
12	The Garden	154
13	Barabbas	165
14	The Beach	172
Postscript		185
References		187

The Power of Your Love
(amended)

*Lord, you come to me,
to help my heart be changed, renewed,
flowing from the grace that I've found,
in you.
And Lord I've come to know,
the weaknesses I see in me,
have been stripped away,
by the power of your love.*

*You hold me close,
you let your love surround me,
you brought me near and drew me to your side.
And as I wait, rising like an eagle,
soaring now with you,
your Spirit leads me on,
in the power of your love.*

*Lord, unveil my eyes,
you let me see you face to face
the knowledge of your love as you live in me.
Lord, renew my mind
as your will unfolds in my life,
in living every day
in the power of your love.*

Acknowledgments

Thank you to:

Dr Ted Boyce for his constant encouragement and input.

John and Jenny Shaw for their love, care and 'open ears'.

Eric and Wendy van Cuylenburg, Michael and Ruth Burgess, Peter and Lois Korf, David and Dale Garratt, Greig and Amanda Whitaker for their friendship, counsel and wisdom.

World Vision Australia for their commitment to the real things of worship.

David and Rachel Dixon of Strand Publishing for this book.

Owen Salter for his fine editing.

Watershed Productions, and in particular Peter and Alison Beveridge, for their constant work in supporting the message of the songs.

To all those who have encouraged us to 'see him' in the midst of our chaos, thank you so much for your grace and love.

This book is a journal from a 'journey of grace'. So many of these 'entries' started life in simple conversations as two pilgrims walked together.

This book is dedicated to my fellow traveller, Victoria. These are our words, yours and mine.

Finally to our children: Nikki, Louise, Joey, Tim, Maddie, Dave and Phil, the greatest grace has been in your love as you walked with us.

To the memory of Garth Ewart, Matthew Boyce and Rachel Pink.

To the praise of his glorious grace.

Introduction

Do you remember the song 'What If God Was One of Us'?

It asked the very simple question: If God was 'one of us', what would you expect of him? How would you react if you knew that he worked in the city, caught public transport to and from the office, went for walks in the park and ate regularly with his friends in his favourite cafe? Imagine if God worked part-time in your office, or served behind the counter of the local butcher shop. As I write, an electrician is replacing some lights in our house. What if he was God? Would that change our concepts? Would that change our spirituality?

If God was one of us, what would he be like?

Would we notice him?

It is amazing that this song was written and its questions asked when people still celebrate Christmas every year. Does this mean that the impact of the true message of Bethlehem has been totally lost on us?

God *was* 'one of us'. He was a stranger walking home along suburban streets every day, passing simple folk just like you and me as they made their way to and from work. He was part of the 'everydayness' of life. He was bumped into, he was sat beside, he was heard, he was interrupted. He was questioned and he was answered. He laughed at other people's jokes, he told stories, he sang and danced. He lived with us, a normal man in a normal world. He had a mother and a father, sisters and brothers, aunties and uncles, friends and enemies. In between the miracles and the teachings was a life just like any other.

How strange. God was a man called Jesus.

As we read about his life, we discover that Jesus came to ordinary men and women as if he was on a mission to find them, personally. He was not found in a large office, served by an army of secretaries with planner diaries and laptops. He wasn't captive to an appointment book full of influential contacts that had been set up for him by a suitably connected public relations firm. Jesus breaks out of the expectations we all have for any important figure. He is the greatest 'figure' of all time, and yet he is the strangest.

> **Jesus is the greatest 'figure' of all time, and yet the strangest.**

He chose the hour of his birth. He chose the town of his childhood. He chose the circumstances that framed his reputation. He walked from town to town as if he was personally looking for people he knew were there. Some he spoke to, some he healed, some he disappointed and some he chose. Those chosen became his disciples. They were not influential, although it does appear that the four fishermen who first followed him were not poor. His disciples were not the graduates of the colleges that raise world leaders, for whatever qualified them for this calling would have rendered them unsuitable to the world.

Jesus comes to us, you and me, John, James, Andrew and Simon Peter. He makes his way, almost unannounced and unnoticed, into our day-to-day living. He joins himself to us, loving us from time eternal past, as we learn the faith to join ourselves to him, as we learn to see him as he really is.

Is it this part of Jesus that makes him so 'unexpected'?

The role we would like God to play is much more public, much more powerful and influential. The Jesus I have heard preached is sometimes like a football star, other times like a

Rambo. I have heard him preached as the great musician (probably preached that one myself), the great conductor, the great charismatic personality who, with one wave of his magic wand, makes everything better so that everyone can live happily ever after. He is the inspiration of songwriters, the subject of books, the answerer of prayers, the bestower of blessings. Jesus has 'spoken' to us through the mouths of evangelists, promising the rewards of 'partnerships'. He is presented as the vindicator, the victory-maker, the fulfiller of all our needs, the one who easily fits into our lives asking nothing more than our tithes (and offerings!). 'He' has led crusades, 'he' has planted bombs, 'he' has murdered dissidents, 'he' has started political parties. 'He' is the most misrepresented historical figure of all time.

We have to prepare ourselves for the true reality of God—the reality that only God can reveal. The Jesus that we have preached may not appear, just as the Messiah that Israel expected refused his supposed role. I find it impossible to believe that we are wise enough to fully describe God. History shows us the opposite. We cannot even agree to love each other, and this is the first evidence of being his disciples! If he came to you and me today, I firmly believe we would struggle with his identity just as much as Israel did.

Jesus, the Prince of heaven, the King of Kings, Bright Morning Star, Emmanuel, Living Word, Holy One of God, Joseph and Mary's boy, walks and talks with those whom every other prince or king would ignore. Jesus serves those whom others would rule. Jesus does not need the affirmation of human beings. He does not court influence. He does not seek popularity. He loves because he genuinely wants the best, even if the best comes at an awful price. He does not flatter, he does not build contacts, he does not even build a kingdom. He is altogether 'un-Godlike'!

He is totally different from what everyone has ever expected him to be, and that is the mystery of the whole gospel!

Every time we expect him to turn to the right, he turns to the left. When we expect him to rebuke, he commends. When we expect him to commend, he rebukes. Those whom we reject he spends the most time with. When we try to bring someone 'important' to him, like the rich young ruler or the religious leaders of his day, he goes to the poor and marginalised. When we try to impress him, we discover that his grace is only found when it is contrasted with our hopeless inadequacy to consistently rise above our nature.

Jesus baffled all who had anything to do with him. He still does.

Jesus baffled all who had anything to do with him. He still does. If he isn't baffling you, you should look harder at who you are expecting him to be. For we all have times when our expectations totally obscure who he really is. Increasingly, this seems to be a crucial part of understanding Jesus and joining his message. We must never stop knocking, asking and seeking. Bono, from the Irish Band U2, put it so simply: 'I still haven't found what I'm looking for.' When we stop looking, we presume that we have found. This book is the continuation of the searchings that began when I realised I knew what everybody else said about Jesus, then searched my heart for the honest answer to the simple question: But do I really *know* him? Looking at him through the lives of those he met, lived with and died for, I began to see that Jesus was not who I expected him to be.

The more I searched, the more I realised that, to Israel and to every generation since, Jesus is 'the Unexpected God'.

1

Interpretations and Expectations

Once upon a time there was a small, insignificant planet in an obscure solar system that orbited a tiny sun. This planet was far more beautiful than any other in the whole universe.

Mountains stretched their snow-capped peaks into clear blue skies. Rocky slopes fell into fertile valleys. Rivers and streams traversed lush landscapes overflowing with trees and flowering shrubs. Grasses carpeted vast plains. Scented flowers bloomed among rocky outcrops, their fragrance filling the air. Great oceans and seas, themselves teeming with life, surrounded the lands like protective barriers, isolating each island's individuality and uniqueness. These seas plunged to great depths, then rose to fall on white sandy beaches and crash on rocky coastlines. They painted the whole planet blue so that when viewed from afar it was an iridescent, multicoloured gem bathed in the light of its sun and orbited by its own white moon.

In vibrant contrast to the vast universe surrounding it, everything on this garden planet was alive. Life burst out of its rocks and soils, its waters and seas. Life, from the tiniest amoeba to the greatest animal, grew from the abundance of this 'Eden'.

This planet bore the signature of a Creator. Its ecosystems and environment, an interweaving interdependence, were designed, purposed and fashioned by the creative genius who filled all the universe, the One who exceeded his creation to such an extent that he could stand back and admire his handiwork as a painter stands back from his artwork. This 'One', this 'God', was beyond comprehension. A God of perfection and purity who created everything—the constellations and galaxies, moons and stars—perfect, complete and ordered. From the largest supernova to the smallest cell, all reflected the beauty and genius of the designer.

And he crowned creation's magnificence with his greatest work: humanity, created 'in his image'.

He then chose to present this reflection of himself with his greatest and most priceless gift. This gift was full of risk, and it was given at great cost. Eternity reeled with the consequences as God gave the irrevocable ability to choose right from wrong, to accept or reject, to reason and interpret. At the very core of this gift was the ability to define all things according to the wisdom that humanity would now independently accumulate, over thousands of years—accumulate until, as frail and short-sighted as it was, humanity would presume itself able to prove or disprove all things, even God himself.

God gave this planet to humanity and humanity lived as ruler over all, cultivating crops, raising herds, populating the earth and defining wisdom. God began to teach humanity as a father would teach his children; but, as all children do, human beings rebelled against the wisdom and principles of their parent. They fought, killed, deceived and connived, distorting right and wrong, abusing the truth and enthroning their lies. Finally they succeeded in the seemingly impossible. Surrounded by an eternity that declared the nature of God, they obscured their Father's likeness.

In the middle of time, this God chose to reveal himself, personally, to his overwhelmingly privileged yet arrogant children. He could have accomplished this in so many ways. He could have written his nature in the clouds, for all to read and marvel at; but he was already spoken of in every created thing, and humankind refused to admit the frailty of its own wisdom. He

Interpretations and Expectations

could have sent a prophet, empowered to speak the truth; but he had already sent hundreds of prophets and they had been disbelieved, persecuted and killed. He could have written songs through the greatest musicians and lyricists, songs that spoke of him, songs that pierced the human soul, bypassing the mind and illuminating the heart. But humanity wrote its own songs and twisted the meanings of God's best efforts.

God had no choice. He came himself in the life of his Son, Jesus.

One would expect humanity to be overwhelmed by the graciousness of this God who came himself, shrinking from the eternal to the finite, clothing himself in our flesh, breathing the dusty air of our world. God gave himself a name so he could be 'called' and 'spoken to'. He had an address so he could be 'found' and 'visited'. He had a voice to speak and hands to touch, a heart to feel and a mind to know. He lived our life with us. He gave himself no advantages, no privileges, no special superhuman quality that set him apart and revealed his true identity. He came alone, unaided, carrying one thing for his journey—his heart of love.

> **God came alone, unaided, carrying one thing for his journey—his heart of love.**

This love was the force of eternity. It held all things together. It was the reason and the foundation for the 'everything of and in' God. It was the only proof that he would offer to his sons and daughters. It would define his identity once and for all, an eternal and absolute statement that identified who he was, what he did and what he expected. He came, a man called Jesus, to love us and live with us, the rich and the poor, all together on this earth. He came serving not ruling, accepting not rejecting.

Human beings, however, chose to exercise the gift that God had bestowed on them at the dawn of time. They examined this God 'made flesh' and, full of their own interpretations and expectations concerning God, lined up Jesus with their own wisdom. They looked from one to the other and then made their final choice.

Expectations determine our sense of place in the world. We meet almost every situation with a predetermined expectation that leads us to either fulfilment or disappointment. If our expectations are fulfilled, they become lifestyles. If, however, they are disappointed, we have a choice: either we re-address our foundations and change our interpretations, or we continue to look for what we expected.

It is easy to see that these fulfilments and disappointments will shape our world view. They will mould every relationship. They will become the foundation of our communications. They will profoundly affect everything we deal with.

Marriage is a result of fulfilled expectations. We look for a partner, a mate. We search our universe for one who will fulfil our desires, our hopes and dreams. One day 'across a crowded room' (or so the song goes) our eyes meet, our hearts skip a beat, and we are pulled by a force that seems stronger than commonsense. Before we know where we are, we have 'fallen'!

Love is in the air and all around us the world is transformed. We have met the one we were looking for, and they have met us. Life has borne us love. Our expectations are fulfilled—in fact, overwhelmed.

Or are they?

Marriages that are surely made in heaven somehow descend into hell. What happened to all the promises? What happened to the vows? What happened to the romance, the roses, the chocolates and the back seat at the movies? What happened to the bridesmaids, the dresses, the flowers, the cars, the photographs, the videos and the expensive honeymoon?

What happened to cause sweet love to sour?

Broken expectations.

Somewhere, somehow, young couples who promised the world to each other and expected the same discovered that they were unable to deliver. They discovered that the one who promised to remain the epitome of romance has turned into the image of humanity—rank (as in smelly) humanity!

Why were we expecting anything else? Didn't we grow up with parents of our own? Surely our mothers and fathers showed us human frailty first-hand. What made us think that 'kissing frogs' would work for us when it was so apparent it hadn't worked for them?

Expectations!

These interpretations shape our lives. They form the foundations for our hopes and dreams and therefore are the building blocks, the operating program, for our future. They become so deeply rooted in us that, by the time we reach adulthood, it takes an absolute personal upheaval to dislodge them.

One of the reasons behind the breakdown of our relationships could be that false interpretations become unfulfilled expectations. The interpretations are wrong, but they remain unchallenged and unchanged—in fact, they are strengthened until they form prejudices that demand conformity or exclusion. They become the ammunition that is hurled between the two warring sides. Absolutes are propelled on the wings of insults as both parties condemn the other's interpretations with their own. Both parties are desperately wounded by broken promises, disillusioned by disappearing dreams. Both insist that the other is to blame. Both seek revenge. Both miss the point as they fight over the spoils.

Reconciliation may only occur as the interpretations are responsibly challenged. When we go back and re-address the very foundations of what we expect from ourselves and each other, we can start to put ourselves and our loved ones back together again.

At the heart of reconciliation, therefore, must be the journey into the insecurity of 'unlearning' what we have mistakenly 'learnt'.

At this point we must discover the truth, because if we don't, we continue to cling to the falsities and frailties of what we believe and what we enforce. When we convince ourselves that 'the other' was at fault, we are in fact refusing to be accountable for our own mistakes. In doing this we assure ourselves of more broken relationships and greater heartache. We will continue to encounter symptoms of the same disease. We will change bandages, hospitals and nurses, but we will never have the courage to look at the wound.

Our lives are built like an American soap. We all hope to meet our perfect match in episode one and marry in prime time at the season finale. We pretend to be Ken and Barbie (we even have operations to look like them). We have a 'Brady Bunch' theology that if we 'do what's right, son, then right will come'. And when we discover the truth that life isn't that simple, we are disillusioned. But we never challenge our illusions. We simply carry them on into the next season, with a new cast and a new set!

Wars have been fought for hundreds of years on the same principles of division. Generation after generation convinces itself that it is the persecuted upholder of the truth and the other side is the 'great Satan'. Both sides sacrifice their young men to their 'truth'. Both sides are convinced of the noble absolute they are defending; and, using the same kind of jargon, they retaliate with the same slogans, simply reworking the words. Both sides expect a 'peace' that is built on the humiliation of the principles of the other, demanding their own absolute 'rightness' and the other's undeniable 'wrongness'.

Nothing ever changes, and the history of the last millennium proves the point. Most of the wars fought today are the result of long-standing disputes that hundreds of years have entrenched in the hearts and minds of multiple generations.

Interpretations and Expectations

It seems to me that the human race is incapable of admitting its own personal wrongs. Even in the face of overwhelming evidence, we will fight to the death rather than admit the obvious.

Is it this inability that is at the core of all our brokenness and disfunctionality? We prefer to feel right and remain dysfunctional rather than be wrong but whole.

If defending our 'rights' causes us to slander, fight, maim and kill each other, surely 'being right' bears fruit that looks altogether wrong. One has to ask the question: Is our 'rightness' that precious? Will its triumph bring a new world order of peace out of war?

We must challenge what we believe. We must prepare for our wrongs to be revealed, because in finding the truth we may also find each other. A community founded on honest admissions of wrong may actually be more peaceful than one that demands its rights.

The interpretations that are established in childhood create the expectations by which we live. When the expectations fail to arrive, we cast off the relationship, blame the other, entrench the interpretation, and redouble our efforts to have our expectations met.

Relationship after relationship after relationship.
Breakdown after breakdown after breakdown.
War after war after war.

For generations political leaders have been voted into office on the expectations of their constituents. These leaders promise that Nirvana will replace disaster the minute they hit office. But the minute they hit office, they 'hit' the previous administration for all the woes they have inherited and declare the promises null and void. Expectations are dashed and the leaders are voted out of office at the very next election. The question the electorate should be asking itself never arises. By making political leaders responsible, the electorate has never become accountable for its false expectations of those leaders and their ability to accept total responsibility and run the country without our help. It is easier for society to blame 'the government' for letting it down.

The electorate also lives under the false understanding that politicians can actually bring immediate change. They are told who is wrong (the government), who is right (the opposition), who can change the mess (the leader of the opposition), and when it will happen (the day after winning government). Sounds like a fairy tale—and we all know that no one lives happily ever after!

And so it goes on.

Communities seek to resolve their differences with the diplomatic tactics of Rambo and then wonder why the blood is real and why both the 'good guys' and the 'bad guys' die horrific deaths.

Churches defend their theological roots by excommunicating brothers and sisters while preaching passionately that 'God is love'.

We long for black–white reconciliation but are so entrenched in our 'rightness' that we are convinced it removes us from identifying compassionately with all the hurts that our unreconciled countrymen still suffer.

Parents sentence their children to fulfil the roles that affirm their own dreams and ambitions. The children fail because they can never live up to these expectations. Little boys are made into 'men' as their natural gifts and abilities are ignored. Little girls are denied the challenges and adventures of their brothers. As this generation grows into adulthood, is it any wonder that they swing to the other side of the pendulum to break the mould of their parents' culture?

Here we are, two thousand years after the greatest portrayal of reconciliation that creation will ever see, and we still haven't learnt the message. We pride ourselves that our society is built on Christian principles, but our world, our nations, our communities and our relationships still remain in such pain and turmoil. No matter what we say about 'the foundations', there still doesn't appear to be any great change or relief in sight.

Until we have the courage to unlearn what we think is 'right' about us and 'wrong' about the other, we will never walk together into a community that can live 'wronged but reconciled'.

Too often we sentence others to live in the shoes that we think they should wear. If they agree to live by our expectations, they will live their lives continually trying to be the person we need them to be. To do this they must surrender their own identity to what we expect of them. They feel trapped and useless, their self-esteem shipwrecked because they are affirmed only when they are esteemed by us. We decide who they are and what they should do, and we remind them constantly of their failure to live up to our standards. In the end, these false interpretations and expectations steal their souls!

Expectations of ourselves cause us the same anxiety. In his book *What's So Amazing About Grace?*, Philip Yancey makes the observation that from early childhood we live in a conditional world. Our relationships in family, school, play and sport all teach us conditional approval. If we 'tidy', 'study', 'excel', 'participate' and 'win', we are accepted. If we don't, we are relegated to the 'bedroom without supper', 'the bottom of the class', 'the lower grade' and 'the empty seats overlooking the sports grounds' (as we become 'the last to be chosen'). Our world becomes conditional, and we expect results according to our performance or lack of it.

We find ourselves trapped in the failure of our own expectations, let alone those of others. We search for meaning. We attend the gym or self-improvement seminars. We make new friends, either because the old friends have rejected us or the new friends offer us an escape. We deal constantly with the symptoms but never address the false concepts of who we are, what we do, and what we need to give us love and acceptance.

False interpretations concerning God lead us into the most tragic consequences of all. When our interpretations of who God is, what he does and what he requires of us are flawed, our expectations lead us further from the truth. We may know grace and mercy, we may sing about love and light, we may know his forgiveness and experience his salvation, but we will live trapped in false expectations of ourselves, false expectations of others, and even worse, false expectations of God.

> **False interpretations concerning God lead us into the most tragic consequences of all.**

We may know that God forgives but still struggle for his acceptance. We may pray harder, study longer, sing louder, believe stronger but still remain unable to accept that his forgiveness and acceptance is unconditional.

Philip Yancey puts it so simply: 'Grace means there is nothing we can do to make God love us more . . . And grace means there is nothing we can do to make God love us less.' If we could really grasp the truth of this statement, all our spiritual performance anxiety would be dealt with permanently.

We feel guilty when we miss a quiet time, especially if the omission is measured in weeks, months or years. We feel second-rate if we can't quote book, chapter and verse. We hide our 'secular' CDs. We may even throw out our old books and cassettes in an attempt to please God—all the while singing the praise of him who loves and accepts unconditionally.

These standards lead us to judge ourselves and others. We strive for spiritual maturity for ourselves by continuing the rituals that we admire in our 'faith heroes' as we watch them climb the ladders of spirituality in the giddy heights above our failed heads. We connect their blessings with their works, and so we too work all the harder, more guilty by the day, as our lives refuse to fit their 'spiritual garments'. We comfort ourselves by teaching these principles to those on the rungs below us. We all suffer without ever questioning whether God has levels of salvation at all.

We live lives expecting more of each other, more of ourselves, more of God, suspecting guiltily that God is expecting more of us. We live a life of 'faith' with all the trimmings of conditionality, and we have never ever had the courage to question it.

The truth about God is far greater than we ever dared to believe.

The more I look, the more I see that this is the issue that must be addressed first. If we can see ourselves as God sees us, then we can start to discover who God really is, what he really does and what he requires of us.

And so God comes in Jesus to show us who we really are and what we really do when our false concepts, and the works that follow, fail. When those who cannot fulfil our expectations are excommunicated and sent packing, we breathe a sigh of relief, believing that we have protected our precious interpretations. We comfort ourselves, reinforcing our laws by confessing that the real problem was never us, it was always those who just 'didn't make the grade'. We cheer each other on, those of us who remain, as we fight the fight of faith, singing all the louder to drown out the cries of the fallen.

In the light of this, Jesus shows us who God is as he becomes the ultimate victim of our judgments. Jesus was killed by us because he refused to perform and respond as expected. He refused to be the Messiah we expected him to be.

Jesus came to this world to show us the truth about God. This truth is far greater than we ever dared to believe, for he was and is totally unlike the person we wanted and expected him to be. He also shows us the truth about us. Here we find the true horror. We are guilty of the greatest crime of all time, and the more we look, the more we find it is not a corporate guilt, it is personal. These two truths demand our response. God leaves that decision to us, proving, to his own cost, that he will not do anything to prevent us from choosing wrongly. He only shows us his love, a love that lives, a love that refuses to die.

We crucify Jesus every time we demand that God perform 'our way'. We crucify him every time we try to make him fit the images we have of him. When we demand this of God—and we do so daily—we yell, 'Give us Barabbas, because God looks so different to how we want to see him.'

But Jesus, the unexpected God, forgave us for crucifying him. He forgave us for choosing Barabbas. He forgave his disciples for betraying him, and he still forgives us as we continue to do the same things.

Forgiveness must be applied to our continual enforcement of our expectations. If we can admit this and grieve for it, we can start to see how deep and constant is his grace towards us. When we see the hammer and nails in *our* hands, then we truly know his unmerited and unconditional grace.

When we realise all that God forgave, we can start to see him as he is, for we can now see ourselves as he sees us.

2

The Grace of His Coming

For unto us a Child is born,
Unto us a Son is given:
And the government shall be upon His shoulder.
And His name will be called
Wonderful, Counsellor, Mighty God,
Everlasting Father, Prince of Peace.
Of the increase of His government and peace
There will be no end,
Upon the throne of David and over His kingdom,
To order it and establish it with judgment and justice
From that time forward, even forever.
The zeal of the Lord of hosts will perform this.

Have you ever thought about the incarnation? Have you ever stopped to think about it—really think about it?

God came to earth as a man!

We humans forget how small we are. We forget the size of the universe. We appear to be ignorant of the greater 'size' of God. We are blissfully unaware of our own insignificance. In fact, it is our own self-awareness that obscures everything else.

The universe contains billions, if not trillions, of stars. These stars are thousands of millions of light years apart. Light years: the distance travelled by light in one year! I was reading recently in a book on advanced astronomy—the Ansett Airlines' in-flight magazine—that scientists are studying a black hole that is thirty million times the size of our sun. A black hole is an imploded star that has shrunk to a fraction of its former size. The gravitational force of this imploded star is so great that even light cannot escape. Makes you ask just how big the star was *before* it imploded! And this is just one black hole in a universe that contains hundreds of black holes. I hope I'm not making you dizzy!

The point of all this is that what we call 'big' is infinitely minuscule.

One clear, moonless night, do yourself a favour and go outside and lie on your back. Look up. You are facing eternity. There is no 'end' to what you see. There is no point where it simply stops. If there was, what then? Wherever you look, a panorama of stars, tiny pinpoints of light, stretches from horizon to horizon. Every pinpoint has travelled for untold years just to have the privilege of falling on your retina! Have you ever thought that if you could be transported to a point two thousand light years from earth, you would be looking at our planet at the time of Jesus? Sounds absurd, and yet this would be comparatively close to us! In fact, comparing this point to the outer limits of the creation, it is right next door!

The more you think about it, the more you realise that our world is so very, very, very tiny.

Why would God even consider this place, let alone need to have any relationship with its life forms? This is indeed more than wonderful. But God goes so much further. Not only is he aware of our address in the back corner of his universe, he is aware of each name that has ever been named. In our quest to know God, we miss the truly remarkable fact that *God knows us*! Whatever you do, don't take this for granted. It is the greatest mystery of all creation. This superb reality defines the character and nature of the Creator of all things. He is not remote. He is not absent. He is not busy elsewhere. There is an eternity of 'elsewheres', but God, for some unfathomable reason, has made humanity the centre of his attention.

Surely we take this for granted.

But this is just the beginning. We are more than 'known'. We are loved. This is mind-blowing. The God who flung the stars into an eternity of space, designing each atom of each molecule of each element from the inside out, building up piece-by-piece to the all that fills all in all—this God, this creative being, this deity of immense intelligence and mind-numbing magnificence . . . this God loves you and me!

If all he did was to send a postcard, or write my name in the clouds just once in a lifetime, that would be enough. But what is enough for me is not enough for God. He goes so much further. He wants me to know his love, to experience his love, and even deeper than that, to know *him*!

Now this brings to mind a strange contradiction. If any of us received a personally autographed message from God, perfectly printed in copperplate twenty kilometres above the Sydney Opera House, we would be pretty impressed. The fact that God has done far more than this, infinitely more, seems to be chronically misunderstood, or even worse, simply dismissed.

God could easily have played fireworks in the sky. He could easily have humbled us with his magnificence and power. He could have done so many 'God-like' things to captivate and bless us. But we would have remained removed and separated from him. We would have retreated into humbled avoidance. Because we could only share our best with this God, we would have to hide the truth from him.

God doesn't need us to love the bigness, the miracles and the splendour. He desires us to love the plain and simple that comes with his heart of love and acceptance.

And so God comes closer. Closer? Just how close can a God get?

> **God has taken steps that totally break all the rules in the book of 'How to Be God'.**

Already he has taken steps that totally break all the rules in the God-likeness book of 'How to Be God'. We should know, because we are the ones who have written all the little rules for God since Adam said, 'What snake? Eve who? It wasn't me!' Already God is appearing 'un-Godly'!

God moves even closer. This now involves us. He desires to come into our personal space—that private part of us that needs to give permission before others can invade.

You know the feeling. You are attending a function of some sort. There are many minglers wandering from group to group carrying a glass of something. One of these minglers moves close to you. Closer to you. Even closer to you. You are backing off and they are advancing, closer. It appears that you cannot escape. You mumble some excuse and retreat to a safe place, where you rebuild your boundaries.

God desires our permission to come this close. He doesn't invade. He knocks. Surely this should be so miraculous that we should be overwhelmed by the immensity of the privilege.

Yet God comes closer!

There is another personal space that is far more private and far more protected. It is the space between our bones, where all our hopes, dreams, ideas and concepts live. We open the outer parts of this space when we feel confident. The more acceptance we feel, the more open we become, and we begin to share the inner things, the secret things, the vulnerable things. When relationships progress to this level we are in dangerous territory. We have opened up to such an extent that we are vulnerable to rejection. We have our whole lives laid out on the table, like an intimate smorgasbord—our prejudices, our quirks, our individuality, our sexuality. Our reality. When this intimacy is violated the consequences are disastrous. Our greatest battles are fought to protect, maintain or re-establish these hard borders that protect and surround the softest parts of us.

God has started his journey from the outer edges of his creation and has aimed for this place. He desires to be the God who knows us, intimately. In between each heartbeat. He comes to be intimate with us. He desires us to be intimate with him. He comes with his borders down, his soul exposed and his vulnerability at stake.

Now we are really touching the character of God. God comes closer to us than we would like. Perhaps you should stop reading for a while and think about this. Ask yourself the question: Has the truth of this great mission of God challenged and changed my concepts of him? Or have I taken it all for granted? The more you recognise who God is and where he could easily be, using all the imagination that you can muster, the more you realise the absolute graciousness of his desire to love and be loved by humankind. To know and be known.

But God goes even further.

He goes further than knowing and loving us. God 'visits' us. He joins us. He becomes part of us.

The incarnation, God becoming human, defines God in such a way that it challenges every thought and concept concerning deity. The royal family travels with kid leather toilet seat covers. World leaders travel in their own planes, with their own chefs. Rock stars refuse to play unless they are provided with a multitude of ego-enhancing paraphernalia. Super models stay in bed unless absurd fees are paid.

God spent nine months inside a Jewish teenage girl!

Why?

Why would God so desire to love us? Why would he have this need of us? Why would he sentence himself to our dusty planet? Why would he suffer with us? Why would he bother? Why would he come?

How deep is this love?

Every night on our television screens we watch scenes of indescribable tragedy and suffering. Kosovo, Bosnia, Sarajevo, Papua New Guinea, East Timor, the list goes on into heartbreak. At the time of writing there are devastating floods in Mozambique. The news footage is damning. Jammed in between advertisements for 'liquid lipstick' and 'protect your wealth portfolios' are scenes of indescribable horror. At this very moment, even as I write, tens of thousands of human beings, with the same feelings you and I have, are clinging to rooftops as rising floodwaters snatch at their bare feet. Thousands will die. Thousands already have.

Imagine if you or I simply stood up from watching the telly, spilling our cafe latte on the floor, and jumped on the next plane to Mozambique. What would people say? What would *you* say to a friend who decided to join these poor people in their suffering? How would you react if your own son's face appeared in tomorrow night's news footage, simply sitting and holding and loving these dying people?

This would be seen as stupidity, compassion gone mad.

God did more.

His actions on our behalf make my last story shallow. His decision to reveal himself to us by coming to live among us makes the greatest act of human compassion comparatively heartless and selfish.

God came to us in the flesh of his Son, Jesus.

Jesus came, compelled by love, propelled by compassion, to write his character into our lives. Jesus joined our story. He jumped out of the pages of scripture, the words of prophecy, the lyrics of the psalms and the requirements of the law. God came to us because every other approach had been misinterpreted. God came to us because we, as humankind, had retreated to the security of our own wisdom and interpretive abilities.

Somehow we have missed the *grace* of his coming. We have been so caught up in our words and wisdom that we have forgotten the true miracle. Our historical images of Jesus have lost their impact. We have reduced his coming to simple Bible stories that are more about carols, mangers, wise men and miracles. We have forgotten the absurd grace of the incarnation while still arguing about our differences.

Imagine the scene in Mozambique if the dying victims of this horrid flood argued among themselves about the reality of the helicopters and the identity of their saviours. Yet our combined collections of corporate wisdom set up boards and authorities that assume the authority to explain God!

Even worse, by assuming who God is, they also have to assume who God isn't.

Somehow, God took this personally and made himself responsible and accountable to set the record straight. Is this because he is offended by our misinterpretations? Is he annoyed by our stupidity, our failure to comprehend? Does he even attempt to correct our ability to receive dictation? No. He doesn't come to argue the words that are written and the conclusions that are made. He comes in a life, not a word. He comes to live, not to be read. He silences all critics by an incarnation that must challenge every interpretation. He does this because we are the victims of our own 'wisdom'. He comes because he loves.

He comes in a life, not a word. He comes to live, not to be read.

God has descended to the human heart. He comes closer to humankind than humankind is to itself. He comes unconditionally to the hurting, the shamed, the loveless, the lifeless, the outcast and the villain. He comes to those we reject. He embraces the unembraceable. He loves the unlovable. He forgives the unforgivable. He offers himself. Not an ideal or a concept. Not theology or apologetics. God comes himself. God comes to know, to feel, to experience, to relate. God comes closer. Instead of taking our vulnerability and shaping it into conformity with his way and his plan, God takes his own vulnerability and, offering it as the priceless jewel that it is, allows us to chose. We can accept and treasure it, or we can use and abuse it, trampling it underfoot. And yet his hand is always open wide, offering, giving, forgiving.

God comes to our heart to show us his heart. He comes to our spirit to show us his spirit. He comes to our lives and, rather than showing us how to live, simply lives with us. We make the choice. We can accept or reject. It will never change who he is.

The vulnerable, intimate God of the universe.

God comes to a human race that has so affirmed its own knowledge of what is 'God-likeness' that it simply refuses to change its mind. Jesus walked among us, the 'unexpected God', the 'unrecognised God'. All that we said about him, all that we did to him, made no difference to who he was. He offered what was continually rejected. He offered it as soon as he was old enough to share it in the temple with the teachers. He offered it for three years, wandering around from town to town like a cast-off hermit. He offered it to unbelieving friends. He offered it to the strong and the weak. He offered it finally to one who had no choice but to accept it, and Jesus and the thief died together—God and the worst of us. They died while his last plea echoed across an unbelieving landscape: 'Father, forgive them, for they do not know what they do.'

Yet even as he pleaded for us to be forgiven, our interpretations made us shove a self-righteous spear through his side so that the dead body of Jesus, God incarnate, would not profane the Sabbath. The Sabbath which was 'holy to the Lord'. The Sabbath where God rested from his labours. The Sabbath where Jesus now 'rested' from his. A Sabbath that would become a memorial Sabbath rest for all.

Now we have two dramatic revelations: who we really are when our interpretations and expectations are challenged, and how God himself responds.

To fully begin to 'see' God we must descend from the awestruck heights of his nature to the sad, barren valleys of humanity's humiliating shortsightedness. I would rather return this narrative to the beauty of creation and the majesty of the unfolding character of God. Let's get caught up in the heavens and leave this world behind. Let's get lost in the moment . . . But that would ignore the way that God is truly revealed to us.

I have found that the more I compare humankind to its Creator, the more I see a gulf that is impassable by any man or woman. The more I search, the more frustrated I feel. I see so much fault in my own life that I marvel that God would bother about me. Then I look at our world and see billions of broken, suffering children, longing for relief. I see the curse of our excuses, the pride of our wisdom, the consequences of our anger and irresponsibility.

And then I look at God, awestruck.

When I begin to see who he really is, realising that I cannot understand any more than a hair's breadth of him, then I must take an honest look at humankind. His grace is defined by his choice to come to us in the light of who we really are and what we really do. God comes to the guilty and the innocent, the victim and the villain. He comes to us all, the perpetrators of hidden violence, self-righteously making tragedies by blaming our victims.

How could God come to this? Because his grace triumphs over it all. His love covers it all.

Only God could go this far.

It proves him to me. Far more than the powerful miracles. Far greater than creation. God absorbs our filth and transforms it, in himself, into grace, mercy and love.

Death into life. A gift, unmerited and undeserved.

How does he do it?

By allowing us to kill him.

Jesus, the unexpected God.

This makes God so much more wonderful than all the majesty and glory of all the praise and worship, all the CDs, videos and rallies. When we see our dust on his feet and his blood on our hands, we truly start to marvel.

God comes to this world so that we can be freed from our false interpretations and expectations. He comes to free us from our need to be right in the eyes of ourselves, the eyes of others and the eyes of God. He comes to challenge our wisdom—to help us begin the journey of disbelief and embrace the insecurity of broken hopes, dashed dreams, false interpretations and failed expectations. God comes as Jesus, who steps away from all our ideas, concepts and expectations and challenges us to know the truth.

God comes to help us embrace the insecurity of broken hopes and dashed dreams.

Jesus asks us the question: What is more important—who we *believe* God is, or who God *really* is?

In Jesus, God came to our planet, a small insignificant part of all that he had created, and stayed. And as we follow his footsteps, we begin to see one thing emerge clearly: Jesus was not who we were expecting.

It is at this point that the truth can be seen. Jesus lived among us, bursting out of our wisdom and words. He can no longer be distorted by us, for he is now seen as who he really is. He is 'highlighted' by the blinding contrast that is now clearly seen in us. The difference between who we say he is and who God reveals himself to be.

Jesus, the unexpected God.

3

The Stage Is Set

Oh, that You would rend the heavens!
That You would come down!
That the mountains might shake at Your presence—
As fire burns brushwood,
As fire causes water to boil—
To make Your name known to Your adversaries,
That the nation may tremble at Your presence!
When You did awesome things for which we did not look,
You came down,
The mountains shook at your presence.

This morning I looked through the book of Isaiah 'without Jesus'. I tried to imagine the hope that these prophecies would have aroused in the most zealous Israelites. I tried to remove the explanation that his life, death and resurrection now brings to these wonderful words, and to expect the fulfilment that *they* longed for.

Imagine walking through occupied Israel. Around you are the many reminders of Israel's captivity. The streets are full of soldiers. Roman standards and banners are everywhere. There is a pervading atmosphere of resentment. Fear stalks every unguarded conversation. Friends have been captured, some put to death. Your heart grieves. You long for the 'former times', the splendour, the glory, the wealth and the power of the kingdom of Israel. The nation was once the envy of the world.

Envoys were sent from every kingdom seeking the favour of your king. God was glorified in the blessings of his children as surely as he is now disgraced. As you walk the streets of Israel, your heart fills with shame as you remember the warnings of the law and the prophets. The former generations ignored these warnings and now judgment has come.

Why this generation? Compared with others, this generation is far more zealous. It has faithfully endured the hard boot of Roman occupation, refusing to 'bow down to Caesar' while remaining faithful to all the law and the prophets. This action alone is fraught with danger, and yet somehow the nation has survived. Surely God can see this? You comfort yourself with the words of Isaiah ringing in your ears as around you oppressed brothers and sisters cry out:

'Justice, mercy, judgment, restoration!'

'Oh God, that you would rend the heavens and come down!'

'God, come and deliver your people from their captivity as you did in the days of old!'

'Send a saviour!'

Before we look at the coming of the Messiah, Jesus, we must walk the streets of Israel. We must attempt to crawl inside the heart of this nation and feel its frustrations and fears. Yearn with the people for the Messiah, live according to their interpretations, join with them in their expectations. It is easy to dismiss their shortsightedness, but only if we also dismiss their pain and shame. If we really want to understand the Israel of Jesus' time, we must empathise. We must feel with them, cry with them, hope with them. We must mourn their martyred sons. We must bathe their scourged backs and comfort their violated daughters. We must join them as they take their frustrations and turn it to faith.

We must long with them for their Messiah—the One they were looking for, the One they were expecting, the One they needed. Then and only then can we look at Jesus and see what they saw. Then and only then we can understand their confused disappointment.

Jesus was born into a climate of expectation. Israel ached for a deliverer. Every generation hoped that it was the 'generation of the Lord'. I can imagine the prayers that were prayed continually for God to come, to have mercy, to deliver and save. The nation had been promised restoration, judgment on her enemies, justice for the oppressed, peace and prosperity for all time. An everlasting kingdom reigning on the throne of David. This nation was expecting salvation.

It would be very easy to superimpose our Western concepts and practices of Christianity onto the Jewish nation at the time of Christ. The language of their spirituality is familiar to us through the Old Testament. Words like 'Saviour', 'Deliverer', 'Messiah', 'Christ' have their place in our own worship, our hymns and songs, our sermons and prayers. To us they speak of the Jesus we know and love, the Jesus of the cross, the Jesus of grace, mercy and love.

But we must never assume the Jews had the same interpretation. They were expecting someone totally different from Jesus.

For them the Messiah had not yet come. All they had was the comfort of their faith and the history of their nation. Their concept of God lay between Genesis and Malachi. Their libraries were full of books that interpreted what God had already said through the law and the prophets. They had the judgment of history to guide them, and it was perfectly clear to every Jewish teacher that this history revealed God to them. It revealed a God who punished the sinful and blessed the righteous. A God who allowed captivity if that would refine the nation.

The Jews were expecting someone totally different from Jesus.

They explained the good, the bad and the tragic in terms of their faith.

We still do the same. God must fit our concepts. God must explain our mistakes. God must be the reason. He must be explained according to our wisdom and knowledge. He must fit into our stories. He must answer our prayers. Sometimes we even demand that he fit into our excuses.

The Israel that Jesus was born into was under a cruel Roman occupation. The history of this little nation spoke of the victories of the 'Armies of the Lord'. Every young Jewish child, every boy and girl, grew up singing the songs of Zion. Generation after generation, the stories of Abraham, Isaac and Jacob were told time and time again. Prayers were offered to the God of Israel, beseeching him to come again as in the days of old. Throughout her troubled history, this nation encouraged each new generation with the law of Moses, the victories of David, the splendour of Solomon, the power of Elijah and the glory of the temple. They were admonished by the years in exile, the accuracy of the prophecies and the judgment on their faithlessness. They practised their worship with a zeal that is still seen to this day at the 'Wailing Wall' in Jerusalem (for Israel still waits for God to come and deliver the nation from her enemies).

Humankind's relationship with God is based on interpretations and expectations. The people of Israel had interpreted God in a way that increasingly defined their expectations.

There were the expectations they believed God had of them. Day after day they would present sacrifices at the temple for the forgiveness of their sins. Day after day they would return home, only to fall again. The law would curse them and they would drag their guilty souls back to repeat the process again and again. Although God had continually revealed himself as gracious, forgiving and loving, they couldn't extricate themselves from the curse that the law brought down on their weary, fallen heads. They lived under a constant cloud of guilt or a fragile confidence that was held together with mind-numbing disciplines.

Their interpretations led them to believe that God angrily expected this from them, and they lived in the fear of failure. Many fell through the cracks. The law had to be defined and redefined to cover every situation. Every part of human life had an appropriate judgment, reward or atoning sacrifice. They couldn't understand a law that was to protect and a grace that was to cover. They needed a law that judged. If the law could declare them righteous, then all they had to do was to live continually by the rules—receiving God's favour and blessings as a result of their works and sacrifices. But if they failed . . . well, then there was nothing left. The gap between the spiritual haves and have nots was cruelly vast.

Sickness was interpreted as a result of sin. Lepers were excommunicated from society. What was it like being sick? How could you deal with the symptoms while being burdened by the fear of God's judgment, especially in an age of barbaric medical practices? The sick must have examined their consciences as their doctors examined their bodies. Guilt stalked every memory. What kind of God did *they* believe in? What kind of God did *they* expect to come? How could they reconcile the beauty of the psalms of David with the hopelessness that awaited them as sickness ravaged their bodies, promising further suffering? What kind of death did they die, when every work, every prayer and every sacrifice failed to remove God's judgment from their flesh? Daily their righteous religious friends admonished them, ignoring the lessons of Job. Daily they endured the rejection that the self-righteous meted out on their heartsick faith as their broken bodies refused to cooperate.

In contrast, the 'spiritual' looked forward to their reward, comforting themselves with their health. They presumed a blessing that was little more than the result of diet, strength and cleanliness.

What kind of 'Messiah' did these two opposing groups expect? The righteous expected blessing. The unrighteous knew they were reserved for judgment—their sick bodies already told them so.

God was also expected to bless the righteousness of the faithful and judge the spiritual poverty of the failed. Many of Israel's religious leaders would have longed for a God who purified the nation of all unrighteousness. They believed the nation was under the judgment of God because of its unrighteousness. Every prostitute and publican would have endured the scorn and moral outrage hurled at them as they were blamed for the nation's fall and cursed with the nation's ills. What kind of God did these outcasts expect?

Then there was the political environment of the time. A nation under cruel captivity must have longed for the God of Elijah. Israel would have remembered the victories of old and promised them to her sons and daughters. Every Roman centurion would have been chilled by the zeal of the Zealots who killed for the glory of Israel's God. Every Zealot would have known compatriots who had died the cruellest of deaths on the Roman crosses that lined the streets into every major city and town. Can you imagine the nature of their 'Messiah'—the deliverer they prayed and longed for as they mourned another friend's death at the hands of Rome? Imagine also the fear that must have plagued any 'spiritual' Roman as he thought of an encounter with Israel's deliverer.

Rome extracted taxes from the population. Cruel, harsh taxes. The nation was oppressed and poverty- stricken, its population on its knees under the economic privation forced on it by the conquering army. You can picture the scenes around the evening table as yet again a family made a meal out of scraps— what prayers were prayed, what songs sung. David wrote, 'You prepare a table for me in the presence of my enemies . . . my cup overflows'. The nation would have longed for the coming of the Lord as much as it longed for his judgment on the tax collectors. What kind of 'Messiah' were they expecting?

The Stage Is Set

Jesus came to answer all these prayers. Jesus came to fulfil the spirit of all the promises made to Israel. His answers, however, were entirely different from the answers they desired.

It is the same in every generation. We believe for God to come, to answer and to help. We pray faithfully, we believe constantly and we hope for what is yet unseen. In our faith pilgrimages we refuse to doubt, we are steadfast in our belief and we wait for him. We long for him. We expect him to come in the image of our prayers, bringing with him our answers, fighting our fights. It is not just Israel that is comforted by the words of Isaiah. Those words apply to all.

Imagine being East Timorese and rejoicing in the election results. Freedom from foreign rule. Freedom from centuries of captivity, governors, colonial powers. Freedom! Independence! Safety! Protection from an angry enemy that has plundered the land. Protection as the rest of the world 'joins hands' through the promises of the United Nations. At last all the prayers have been answered. The tears have been seen. Justice has come.

Jesus came to fulfil all the promises to Israel, but his answers were entirely different from the answers they desired.

Your heart races! You dance in the streets!

Now imagine the horror, the isolation and the desolation of the next three weeks as 'freedom' descends from an unexpected heaven to an unprotected hell. The priests are murdered and the churches are burnt. The cities are on fire and the men are all gone. The hills become a refuge as fear stalks every street. Your protectors hide in their fortified camp while the 'eyes' of the world's media leave in droves. Every morning the promise of help is overpowered by the brutality of the day. Your wells are full of bodies. Your houses are gone. Your saviours in their white Landrovers, with their international flags and their promises of protection, are flying away. You are left without hope, isolated, ignored and alone.

Read Isaiah as if it was written for you, abandoned in East Timor, and comfort yourself with his words ringing in your ears as around you oppressed brothers and sisters cry out:

'Justice, mercy, judgment, restoration!'

'Oh God, that you would rend the heavens and come down!'

'God, come and deliver your people from their captivity as you did in the days of old!'

'Send a saviour!'

What would you expect of your 'Messiah'?

Now imagine your great, great, great, great grandfather crouching in waste deep water with a spear in his hand, his eyes piercing the pristine shallows of a rocky shore. This is his land, the land of his fathers and their fathers before him. This land is his story. His spirit is in the land, the spirit of the land is in him. They are 'one nation'.

He looks up from his fishing. He has been startled by the cries of the elders of his camp. They are pointing across the water. His heart recoils in fear and horror as he sees great white apparitions floating on the waves. They draw nearer. He looks again and the apparitions have turned into billowing white clouds that gather in uniform shapes around tall trees growing out of impossibly big canoes. There are figures in the canoes. They look like ghosts, white-faced ghosts, or spirits of ancient warriors. They are wearing colourful skins and carrying polished sticks. They beat on drums. They line up as if for battle or ceremony.

They draw closer. Your great, great, great, great grandfather searches his mind for a story that would explain this. He is petrified. He is awestruck.

The ghosts drop anchor and come ashore. They are men. The ghosts stay—and destroy his land, poison his waters, scatter his tribe and kill his brothers and sisters. (No wonder it is called 'Invasion Day'.)

Now imagine the rest of your great, great, great, great grandfather's life and then read Isaiah as if it was written for his tribe and his land. Comfort your ancestor with the comfort of Isaiah's words ringing in your ears as around you your oppressed brothers and sisters still cry out:

'Justice, mercy, judgment, restoration!'
'Oh God, that you would rend the heavens and come down!'
'God, come and deliver your people from their captivity as you did in the days of old!'
'Send a saviour!'
What would you expect of your 'Messiah'?

Both East Timor and Australia lie under the Southern Cross. Both nations had God's story in their skies. Long before there was an Indonesia or an England, an Israel or a Rome, this Southern Cross promised, to all who looked skywards, the coming of Jesus, the fulfilment of the words of Isaiah. Throughout the centuries of tragic, inhumane history, East Timor, Aboriginal Australia and the Israelites in captive Israel had the same promises of Isaiah to give them hope, for they were written for these as much as they were written for Israel. 'The heavens declare the glory of God.'

Israel, awaiting the birth of God's Messiah, was not the only nation with hopes and dreams of deliverance.

But God was not imprisoned by those hopes and dreams. In the eternity of timelessness, seeing the suffering of every generation from the first breath of Adam till the last night of earth, he inspired the prophet to write about his Son. Jesus is God's finest moment—his salvation for humankind. Jesus is *God's* 'answer', reaching out in love to heal his creation and to teach us to be healers in his name, his love and his life.

As we now combine all Israel's 'longings'—the prayers, the songs, the hopes, the promises of Isaiah—we may also become aware of some of our own. As we look around and struggle with all that we see, surely we wish and pray for a God who would judge the wrongs, right the wrongs and restore the rights of the wronged—a God who would 'rend the heavens and come down'. Maybe our expectations, like every generation in every nation before and since the birth of Jesus, demand that he conform to our needs, our desires and our image of him—who we need him to be.

God must either answer us the way we want, entrenching our beliefs, or refuse to answer, entrenching our unbelief.

It is clear that Jesus never accepted any challenge to conform or explain. He knew who he was and refused to submit to the image of our expectations. In our struggles for mercy and justice we now must struggle with our perceptions. Has God the ability in this 'Son of God' to meet the stark realities of our lives and our world? We can 'fit' Jesus into our church life, but can he break out of our pews and triumph over the personal tragedy of an East Timorese widow? And what answer do we find in Jesus in a nation that is too proud, too removed, too complacent or too bigoted to simply say the word 'sorry' and live accountable to the past?

We struggle with our answers. It is easier to justify ourselves by 'blaming' God. God must either answer us the way we want, entrenching our beliefs, or refuse to answer, entrenching our unbelief. Either way, we try to prove ourselves and our concepts by placing God in a box and then answering on his behalf. This box has an inscription, in our handwriting: *Identity of God*. When God dares to 'jump out' (or even worse, refuses to 'get in') we have a problem.

'*Mum, God won't play by my rules! Can I send him home? I really like my rules. I don't want to change them. Mum, tell God to play by my rules!*'

Why is it that we continually try to change God? When our concepts are challenged by his stubbornness to play ball, we fall back, struggling with our 'creeds'. We go back to the rule book, to our wisdom, to our interpretations and the words of others. We look at Jesus, puzzled by what we see as inconsistencies. We then attempt to re-explain him.

At some point our desires become so desperate and our beliefs so entrenched that we refuse to consider that we may be wrong. We interpret God's will and then enforce it, demanding that God respond to our version of his words. We refuse to allow him to be any bigger than a verse or line. We make the will of the Creator of the universe subject to our interpretation. We place all our hope and faith in what *we* believe he does and who *we* believe him to be. Look at the history of God, as he progressed (in our understanding) from altars to arks to tents to temples. When Jesus died, the veil separating God from humanity was ripped from top to bottom, but we have spent two thousand years putting God back into the pages of a book.

Now before you howl and protest, let's all recognise that scripture is God-breathed. But let's also recognise that God is bigger than his words, just as an author is bigger than his autobiography.

When God refuses to do what we expect of him, do we place our disappointments at the feet of Jesus and challenge our interpretations? Or do we wave our Bibles in his face and demand, 'It is written'?

Jesus came to a nation that was fanatically immersed in its own disciplines, its own concepts and its own hopes. Israel cried out daily, hourly for God to come and deliver. And Jesus came to answer those prayers. He came personally. And yet they scratched their heads because he didn't fit their pages. He was not the illustration they were looking for.

Are we the same? Are our concepts interpreted for us by Christ, or is Christ interpreted by us through our concepts?

There is an eternity of difference, and the cross is the final proof.

We want our beliefs to be affirmed. We want our prayers to be answered. We want our kingdoms to come. And sadly, in the end it is our will that we want Christ to do.

Every generation is waiting afresh for the revelation of God. Every heart must come through its own journey of unbelief. We have a choice. Either our hopes will be disappointed or they will be superseded.

Jesus comes to answer our prayers. But he comes with *his* answers. He comes himself, as Life, a living Word that must burst out of the pages of our interpretations. Whether we recognise him or not simply depends on 'who we are waiting for'.

Israel was waiting. They were desperate for a Messiah, a deliverer, a saviour, a redeemer and a king.

They were expecting him. They had much for him to do.

4

Nazareth

Who has believed our report?
And to whom has the arm of the Lord been revealed?
For He shall grow up before Him as a tender plant,
And as a root out of dry ground.
He has no form or splendour;
And when we see Him,
There is no beauty that we should desire Him.
He is despised and rejected by men,
A Man of sorrows and acquainted with grief.
And we hid, as it were, our face from Him;
He was despised, and we did not esteem Him.

The morning service has just finished. Children have started running around the hall. The morning's notices are being hurled around as little boys make paper aeroplanes out of a hard week's work by the church secretary. Parents are trying to catch up with other parents. Mums are steering their prams through the jungle of teenagers playing follow the peer group leader.

Someone has put on a worship tape, but it is struggling to be heard above the din created by the little boy playing the drums. The musicians are packing up their instruments, trying to escape from the noise. Groups of young people are already plotting to take over McDonald's for lunch. Mothers have rescued the creche coordinators from the clutches of their mutinous children. Surrounded by it all, the pastor is breathing a sigh of relief. His sermon didn't go overtime and cause a dozen roasts to burn. He is doing his best to tolerate—graciously, of course—the same old lady whose name slipped his mind last week as she instructs him on the finer points of 'enduring old ladies'. The car park is a chaotic circus of teenage boys on skateboards and cars negotiating the chicane created by groups of flirtatious teenage girls trying to avoid being seen by the teenage boys as both groups do their best to be noticed.

Inside the church, the usual young suspects are playing soccer with an offering container that the treasurer is hoping was empty. It bounces around the feet of the young couples arranging the day's social activities and narrowly misses the youth pastor as he practises his earnestness (after all, he is preaching tonight!).

There is an animated conversation going on in the back corner and curiosity gets the better of you. You work your way within earshot. The conversation centres around the appearance of a new ministry. It sounds fascinating, and you are just wondering how you can graciously insert yourself into the discussion when suddenly someone says something that sets your 'alarm bells' ringing . . .

We have all become attuned to 'spiritual alarm bells'. They sound every time we sense 'in our spirit' that something is 'not of God'. If you listen very carefully, you can hear them go off every Sunday morning. In fact, I have become quite an expert at 'discerning the alarm bell spirit'. The best way to tell is not to listen at all, or at least not at first, but to watch. (It's always better to watch than to listen; I think they teach that at Bible College!)

Try it yourself next Sunday. Watch one of the more 'serious prayer warriors' in your church. You won't have to wait long before they make a quizzical expression—something like the one you would make if you accidentally trod in something obnoxious and swore off dogs for life. This is where the listening comes in. What noise immediately preceded the expression? Let me make it easier for you. It usually has something to do with:

A. The drummer.
B. The long-haired guitarist.
C. The sound operator.
D. All of the above.

After you have observed all this regularly, you too will become an expert in spiritual 'alarm bells'.

Usually it is not until the third half of the sermon that these bells really start to ring. Everyone knows that the third half is one half too many and that the pastor has just 'lost the anointing'. Sometimes they go off in the car park when a certain young man places his ego-machine in your parking space. I have found that they never go off when you are alone.

Funny about that.

We have, deep inside our anointed spirits, a 'Big Ben'. This only chimes when there is a threat of nuclear war, holocaust or Armageddon. And its large, serious chimes ring like a cheap alarm clock at anything that sounds like: 'The Antichrist!' Your spiritual 'Big Ben' just chimed thirteen. You heard the dangerous words that clear churches faster than you can say 'building program'.

'A lot of people reckon he's the Messiah.'

Everyone is laughing and telling their favourite 'cult story'. At the center of the group is a young man whose face is growing redder by the moment. He is not laughing. He is serious. His voice rises shrilly above the giggles, the rolling eyes, and the racket of all those bells:

'But he's God. Come and see for yourself.'

'Who is he? Where is he from?' comes the chorus of replies.

'He's from a small country town in north-west Queensland. He's a carpenter.'

Would *you* believe?

Would *you* believe that God would send a Messiah to some place west of Mount Isa?

Has a nice ring to it, doesn't it?

> **Would *you* believe that God would send a Messiah to some place west of Mount Isa?**

In the days when Jesus started his ministry, this conversation happened daily. As his ministry grew in influence and reputation he was the talking point in most religious circles.

Israel was expecting a Messiah. But were they expecting Jesus? Let's look at the evidence.

The first questions asked would be:

'Who is he and where is he from?'

'Who is his family? How did he grow up?'

The answers would presumably bring credibility to his message and silence the bells forever.

We would expect God's Son to have a glorious past and a wonderful childhood. He would be the toast of the town, the man voted 'Most Likely to Succeed'.

Surely?

To answer this, we firstly have to unlearn all our romantic ideas about the birth of Jesus.

In my first book, *Hands of Grace*, I explored in some detail the birth and early life of Jesus. In writing this I discovered that the 'fairy tale of Bethlehem' was not what it seemed. Many things stood out. Mary received a message from an angel. She was pregnant to God! She sang a song, and then what did she do? She ran away to her cousin Elizabeth! Nazareth to the Judean hills is not down the road. It is the other end of the country. I have visited both places by bus, and believe me, it is not a simple stroll. Mary was a teenager. As far as Nazareth was concerned, she just disappeared! Three months later, just when all the rumours had stopped, guess who walked back into town, unannounced? A pregnant Mary, with only her story to protect her. Even Joseph had to be restrained by an angelic visitation.

Not a great start to impressing the in-laws!

In October 1999 my wife and I visited Nazareth as part of a tour we were hosting. Nowadays Nazareth is a large, bustling Palestinian town in the hills above the Megiddo Valley. Big international hotels catering for the tourist shekel rise above a myriad of shops selling everything that a tourist bus full of pilgrims doesn't really need. The 'holy site' of the annunciation is covered by a huge cathedral. Very impressive. People, bikes, markets, buses, tourists, hustle and bustle.

Our guide started his 'Introduction to Nazareth' story, no doubt for the umpteenth time. But his first words rocked me. I thought I knew. I'd written a book on the subject! I thought I was an authority! Funny how I could think these things when I hadn't even seen the place before, but such is human pride.

The guide simply said, 'When Jesus lived here, this was a very small village containing only about twelve families.'

This changes everything about Mary's story. Think about it.

They lived in a town of relatives. A close-knit community that knew everything about everyone else. Mary was engaged to Joseph. Wonderful! Everyone in Nazareth knew Mary and her family. Everyone knew Joseph and his. These two kids had grown up watched by the whole village. They had probably stayed the night in just about every house in town. The local synagogue ruler knew them. The village elders were consulted about the engagement. A wedding was a community event, so plans must have been underway. And then suddenly Mary disappeared!

This is a horror for any town, but for a small, tight-knit community in the Galilean hills it would have stopped the whole village. The whole extended family from both sides, Mary's and Joseph's, would have been grief-stricken. Joseph would have searched high and low for his bride to be. The Megiddo Valley and the surrounding hills would have echoed with his plaintive cry: 'Mary! Mary!' Everything that everyone knew became everyone's business as this small town came to grips with an unexpected family tragedy. They were expecting a celebration, a wedding, a party. They would have had a memorial service instead.

And then after three months Mary returned—visibly pregnant.

Would you be happy to see her?

There is no mention of a wedding in the Bible. Joseph's grief, anger and suspicion was dealt with in a dream, and by his great love. He had a choice, remember, but the villagers—what did they say?

It is a miracle that Mary and the unborn Jesus survived. All I can imagine is that the elders and the synagogue ruler adopted a 'wait and see' mentality. They sat on the fence. If Mary was being truthful, they couldn't possibly think of stoning her; they would have the blood of the Messiah on their hands. If she was lying, the child would prove it, and they could deal with her later. Best to do nothing. Don't hinder and don't help.

By the time Mary was to give birth, she and Joseph were absolutely alone. They travelled to Bethlehem to register for the census. Why were they alone in Bethlehem? There were plenty of relatives around—the whole town was related that night. Joseph's father, uncles, cousins and brothers (if he had any) would have been there. Joseph's mother would have accompanied her husband. After all, this was the greatest 'homecoming' this generation had ever seen.

Joseph and Mary, however, were turned away from house after house, by relative after relative. The innkeeper, presumably another relation, showed them the back door to the back shed. And there Mary, frightened, alone and inexperienced, gave birth to the child that was the cause of all the fuss.

What homecoming awaited them in Nazareth? What 'proof' did the village demand to absolve this young couple from their sinful relationship? Perhaps Joseph was believed, but what proof did he require from his new bride? What did they all expect of the child?

Perhaps Nazareth waited in some anticipation, for if the story were true they were about to become the centre of national attention. The synagogue may have been swept and cleaned. The synagogue ruler may have had new garments made as he prepared his 'welcome to Nazareth, birth place of the Messiah' speech. No one knows the thoughts that went through the villagers' minds, but we are sure of one thing: they eagerly awaited the return of this infamous couple and the child of so much controversy.

But they waited a long time, because (as they saw it) Mary 'did another runner'. The story would have gone something like this: 'True to form, Mary has repeated her mistakes. She's run away again. This time she's taken poor Joseph with her and her abominable illegitimate child. Poor love-struck, foolish Joseph. What did he do to deserve such shame?'

Now *we* know the truth. God sent an angel to warn them of the plans to kill Jesus, and they escaped to Egypt. However, all that Nazareth heard was silence. Silence and small town, small-minded rumour, innuendo and judgment.

After many years, just as Nazareth had forgotten this shameful part of its past, just as both families had overcome their grief, anger and humiliation, guess who walked back into town? Would Nazareth rejoice and throw a party? After all that had been said and done, after all the pain and shame, would the return of Joseph, Mary and Jesus be good news?

We must think about these things, otherwise the crucifixion doesn't make sense.

What did Joseph and Mary think as, year after year, nothing distinguished their 'child of promise' from any other child in town? What were the rumours flying around behind young Jesus' back as, year after year, Mary's story failed to bring forth any evidence in the life of her son? What did Jesus' brothers and sisters have to say about the turmoil they were born into? Did they resent this child who either just plain refused to reveal his true identity, or couldn't? Did Joseph and Mary pray for God to send another angel to take away the family's reproach? What was it like for the young Jesus? Was he teased? What was his relationship like with Joseph's family? Did he ask why they weren't at his birth? Did he have friends? Was he aware of the controversy that surrounded him?

Every year the village would go up to Jerusalem for the Feast of the Passover. Perhaps Mary and Joseph would get together with her cousin Elizabeth and her husband, the priest Zacharias. Perhaps every year Elizabeth and Zacharias would ask if there was any sign. Year after year there was none. Were these visits comforting for Mary and Joseph, or did they increase their frustration? Perhaps each year they expected a sign in Jerusalem. Perhaps God would answer. Year after year, feast after feast, they trod the miles to the Holy City and back again, accompanied by an increasingly cynical village.

One year they left Jerusalem and travelled for a day before they noticed Jesus was missing. I've travelled the road from Jerusalem to Galilee; the first day or so is through the wilderness to Jericho. The road winds down through bare, rocky hills. Mountain goats cling precariously to impossibly steep slopes. It was in this wilderness that John the Baptist started his ministry. It was in this wilderness that Jesus withdrew for forty days and forty nights. And it was in this wilderness that Joseph and Mary realised that Jesus had been left behind.

Don't you think that someone else would have asked where he was? Or maybe the rest of the touring party had presumed that Mary had finally done the 'right thing' and left the boy behind as an offering at the temple. In any case, they turned around and retraced their steps, uphill, back to Jerusalem. The road that leads from Jericho to Jerusalem was very dangerous in those days. Pilgrims were ambushed constantly by bands of robbers. This small group of people from the north, rough, unsophisticated country folk, trod the dangerous paths as they went to 'save' the boy.

What was their conversation, especially after Jesus did not appear to be in any way contrite or apologetic? His reply to his parents' horrific ordeal was: 'Why did you seek me? Did you not know that I must be about my Father's business'?

He was twelve! So is my second son. My response would have been swift and to the point. What on earth did Joseph and Mary do? What did they say as again they negotiated the dangerous wilderness down to Jericho and then went along the Jordan River to Galilee and up the hills to Nazareth? What did they say to their relatives, family and friends as they all trod mile after mile?

Year after year went by and there were no proofs. No angelic visitations. The life of Mary's son was the same as his relatives' sons. He was a normal boy. He was a man. He was not God.

He was just the carpenter's son.

What was said during those years as Joseph and Mary and their family—Jesus, his sisters and his brothers James, Joses, Judas and Simon—gathered around the family table? (It is interesting to note that during Jesus' later ministry his family was conspicuously absent, except for a few instances.) How was 'the story' dealt with as they ate together with the teenage Jesus? How did Jesus come to grips with the growing awareness of whose Son he was and whose son he was thought to be?

How did Jesus come to grips with the growing awareness of whose Son he was?

How did Nazareth get over the scandal? Did it get over the scandal?

The Bible is silent about all these issues, except for a simple verse in the Gospel of Luke:

And Jesus increased in wisdom and stature, and in favour with God and men.

God's favour was obvious. Jesus was his Son. The favour of the people was a far different thing. God's favour was unconditional, the people's was not.

As Jesus grew into a man, the story of his conception and birth perhaps faded. He would have 'proved' himself as he simply lived and worked as Joseph and Mary's son. Perhaps he indeed gained favour as his wisdom and stature grew in Nazareth. But whatever Nazareth thought of Jesus, it must have been conditional on Jesus 'playing his rightful part', because one day that favour turned into hatred as he stepped outside the boundaries of his town's expectations.

Yesterday's political leaders, cricket captains, presidents and Internet stocks are thrown away in disgust when they cease to fulfil the expectations of their devotees.

Thirty years after the pregnant Mary walked back into town, carrying a child that perhaps the whole village had determined was illegitimate, this child returned again as a man. He came to answer his mother's cry for vindication. He came to bring proof.

Jesus went to the synagogue in Nazareth and stood up to read from the scriptures. He looked around at a room full of familiar faces. They knew him. They all believed that they 'knew' the truth. Jesus, with thirty years of barely buried suspicion sitting in front of him, read:

The Spirit of the Lord is upon Me,
Because He has anointed Me
To preach the gospel to the poor;
He has sent Me to heal the brokenhearted,

To proclaim liberty to the captives
And recovery of sight to the blind,
To set at liberty those who are oppressed;
To proclaim the acceptable year of the Lord.

They knew this passage. The whole nation longed for its fulfilment. There should have been rejoicing in the streets. Our home-town boy is the Messiah! Mary was right! It's true! The news should have been too glorious, too wonderful, too marvellous for words.

Jesus went further. Perhaps he emphasised the word 'me' while he was reading, and now he made it crystal clear. He looked into their faces again. Every eye returned the stare. He knew them all by name and they knew his name. Just before they could tell him, he beat them to it:

'Today, this scripture is fulfilled in your hearing.'

As soon as the words were out of his mouth, the villagers responded. Yes, his words were gracious, but:

'Is this not Joseph's son?'

Was it all too much for unsophisticated Nazareth? Had too much water passed under the bridge since Mary's story? Had they had enough of this boy?

What went through the minds of those who were in the synagogue that day as Mary's son brought back all the memories of the unfinished business concerning whose child he really was? It is clear that they hadn't believed her story all along because their reaction now revealed years of pent-up anger, years of frustration as their self-righteous hands were tied by family loyalties. This boy had left town too many times to return again with another story. Enough was enough.

They were filled with wrath, and rose up and thrust Him out of the city; and they led Him to the brow of the hill on which their city was built, that they might throw Him down over the cliff.

Whatever Nazareth was expecting from Mary's son, they didn't see it in Jesus. Perhaps his presence was barely tolerated. Maybe the 'old guard' had long memories. But all at once, what had simmered for years exploded. Nazareth was in uproar. Jesus had said the unthinkable. He had the insolence to believe the absurd. He had the absolute gall to throw it back into the faces of those who had 'protected' his mother all those years ago. Didn't he know his place? Didn't he know the truth? Why hadn't they acted as they should have when Mary first told this lie?

Please forgive me for this, but it may help us to understand the reactions of Jesus' family, friends and relatives in Nazareth and the reaction of all Israel, particularly in Jerusalem on the eve of the Passover a few short years away.

All Nazareth knew the truth. They had hidden it from the outside world as they 'protected' the story of Joseph and his wife, the much-maligned Mary. They had suffered as a village under the weight of the shame and guilt. They had argued about it. They had debated it, deciding to let the boy's life prove the story—and it hadn't. There was no evidence to support Mary's tale about an angel, a star, shepherds, wise men and visions. Poor Joseph had been duped all along until he too believed it. They were not going to let it continue. If this got out, everything they had done to keep it in would be in vain. The town would be humiliated. How could Jesus treat them this way, after all they had done for him? They had tried to forget. They had

Jesus had said the unthinkable. He had the insolence to believe the absurd.

tried to give him their favour. He owed them his life, and now he repaid them by completely losing his senses. Even his family was thought to have doubts.

Israel was longing for a saviour. Nazareth was longing for a saviour. But Nazareth knew it wasn't Jesus. Why? Because all Nazareth knew that he was:

'Jesus the bastard!'

They took him by force to the edge of town. They grabbed him roughly, the young men taunting him, the old men humiliated by his ingratitude. They found the best and highest cliff that was worthy of his blasphemy. They had every intention of finishing this once and for all.

Yet somehow, Jesus simply subdued their anger. At the high point of their judgmental rage, he simply walked through this angry crowd of former 'friends' and left town.

His time had not yet come, no matter what Nazareth thought.

5

Arise, Shine

Arise, shine;
For your light has come!
And the glory of the Lord is risen upon you.
For behold, the darkness shall cover the earth
And deep darkness the people;
But the Lord will arise over you,
And His glory will be seen upon you.
The Gentiles shall come to your light,
And kings to the brightness of your rising.

Jesus' neighbours, the very ones who had watched him grow from baby to boy, boy to man, could not break away from their initial prejudices and predetermined concepts. They withdrew their favour and replaced it with indignant scorn. They 'knew' who Jesus was all along, and now, in the light of Jesus' own actions, they were not prepared to question or challenge that absolute.

They also 'knew' who the Messiah should be. And although this was not as fixed as their judgment concerning Jesus, both concepts were as far away from each other as Gentile from Jew and saint from sinner.

Their rage and indignation settled the matter once and for all. But what turned a morning's reading in the synagogue into a lynch mob on the outskirts of town? Jesus read from Isaiah and announced its fulfilment. This should have been glorious, an announcement that awakened hope and promoted peace. What happened to turn the village against its 'son'?

I'm sure you've heard the phrase 'I'll forgive, but I'll never forget'. It is a well-used platitude that really says, 'Let's move on. I'll hide my feelings, but don't ever think that you'll get away with what you've done.' This phrase sets the boundaries that forever sentence one person to be the victim and another to be the villain.

It is important to realise that we are all victims of each other's villainy. Unfortunately, very few conflicts end with this understanding. If they did, there would be far fewer wars. In our fragmented processes, the victim 'frees' themselves from responsibility for their actions and 'moves on'. The villain is left with the sentence of total responsibility, never moving on, always beholden to the judgment of the victim and their friends. Both have to deal with the ensuing disfunctionality as they apply this process of denial and blame, bandaging an increasingly festered wound while living in a world where forgiveness is as brief as memories are strong. There is a time bomb ticking away, hidden in the unforgetting recesses of each hurting heart. Its fuse is lit every time the wounds are touched.

Jesus touched the wounds of Nazareth and the bomb went off with such fury that all the hope of salvation was smothered by damnation. Jesus dared to reinterpret their disappointment. He dared to challenge their preconceptions. He dared them to challenge their own expectations concerning both him and their 'Messiah'. He dared them to open again the story of his mother, and once and for all see it for what it really was: the 'hour of their visitation'.

That day, two simple questions rang out from Nazareth, echoing across all creation until they challenged heaven to its core: how could he? and how could they?'

One interpretation or the other had to change.

It is here that the Nazareth we 'see' historically must be

applied to our day. We must broaden our reactions to include ourselves.

Nazareth was so intent on enforcing its 'truth' that it was never brave enough to challenge that 'truth' for itself. Our Christian world is much the same. We defend our theological interpretations, judge our world's morality and preach along the lines of our expectations. We build our churches with the 'dirt' of Nazareth—not mud-bricks and mortar, but the same resolute determination to define God, defend God, admit God and excommunicate God. Jesus has to fit our concepts, and only then do we preach him to the world. We reinforce the frailty of our limited wisdom, presuming God's agreement. We never consider the possibility that we may be demanding that he 'reinvent' himself in order to conform to our needs and our image of him.

Having backed God and ourselves into this inflexible corner, we bar the windows and lock the doors. Then we live by our own light, too scared to admit that we may have been wrong all along. In fact, being wrong is unthinkable.

Nazareth missed her greatest day. Nazareth was locked into the shame that had been inflicted on the village from the moment young Mary disappeared. This shame flowed from the villagers' own interpretation of Mary's story. Their pain was as real as it was unnecessary, and it increased each time the truth was interpreted as a lie. It increased each time Mary's son refused to play his part and reveal the 'truth'. Jesus either had to admit his illegitimacy and become an outcast, or perform and fulfil their expectations of God. Nazareth was never prepared to admit the third option—that Jesus was God in the flesh and they were wrong.

How many times do we all come to this point?

So here again we face the most marvellous yet painful decision. We are on the verge of the greatest revelation. We are about to discover the true identity of God. In discovering this, we will also discover who we really are and what we have really done to the message of Jesus. But we have to remove the 'bandages' and address the 'infection'. The source of the infection is our need to be 'right'. We want to find the 'correct revelation' so that we can prescribe the 'correct response'. Then we can congratulate ourselves on finding the truth all by ourselves. This 'truth' then becomes the 'bandage' we offer our broken world.

Jesus, however, came to Nazareth to remove these religious bandages and bathe our wounds with unconditional love and acceptance. Jesus came to render our bandages obsolete by declaring our 'doctors' as sick as their patients.

We can look at the wounds of our false expectations—wounds that injure both our broken souls and God's revelation of himself—so that we see the truth without prejudice. Or we can retreat to the comfort of communal wisdom and deny the reality of God, the reality that Jesus came to reveal in Nazareth.

Do we wrap our broken dreams with tighter bandages, or do we allow God to take us back to the truth of our 'sicknesses'? Healing will come as the reality of the real truth sets us free. Jesus came to a world lost in its sicknesses. The glaring gap between the 'good' and the 'bad' was invisible to Him. He came to those who were sick and joined them. He then called to their 'doctors' to admit that they were no different. When we all, doctor and patient, teacher and pupil, admit that our bandages are self-righteous rags, we can then have the absolute joy of seeing him as he really wants to be seen.

Jesus came to remove our religious bandages and bathe our wounds with unconditional love and acceptance.

The people of Nazareth had the choice. They made their decision and tried to kill the truth so that they could keep the bandages.

If Nazareth had chosen the other way, think how wonderful it would have been:

Arise, shine *Nazareth*;
For your light has come!
And the glory of the Lord is risen upon *you*.

But they would not choose. The tragedy of this is overwhelming.

What was Jesus saying to them in the synagogue that day? What was 'between the words'?

Jesus was addressing their concepts of God. He wasn't trying to teach God to them through the words of Isaiah or bring some spiritual incantation that suddenly removed the scales from their eyes. They knew the words. But now the words had to 'become flesh' as they were applied to him. In the mind of God, the passage Jesus read fitted him like a glove. In the minds of the generations after Isaiah, however, the 'fitting' had changed. Now it had to be remade and altered to once again fit Jesus.

This was no easy task. To turn around a small town attitude concerning its infamous son was daunting. To change a nation's expectations concerning the prophet Isaiah's words was nigh on impossible. This is the challenge that faced the synagogue in Nazareth that morning as Jesus read from the scriptures. This is the challenge that faces all who hear familiar scriptures read again and again.

Jesus the carpenter's son stood before the people who thought they knew him best and, in an act of absolute vulnerability, said the truth. If they believed him they would come to the wonderful realisation that the fulfilment of Isaiah's prophecy had been unfolding right before their eyes for thirty years. All Jesus' life, Nazareth had demanded that he 'change'; now the reality would dawn that it was Nazareth that had to change. What a daunting thought. They couldn't face it.

What can we learn from Nazareth? It all goes back to the questions 'who was he?' and 'where was he from?'

Jesus was the son of Mary and Joseph and he came from Nazareth. God chose the people of this tiny country backwater because their reactions to Jesus' true identity would highlight God's true message of salvation and deliverance. He chose an unmarried virgin and the reactions of her family and neighbours to her 'illegitimate' son. And as they finally and prophetically vented their fury on Jesus, the message was complete:

> **Jesus reinvents our God for us, presenting him back to us: 'his image in our flesh'.**

'I am the God who joins you in your pain and shame. I come to taste your tears and frustrations. I will live with you through the nights of broken dreams. I will comfort you when all have turned away. I will stand beside you at the graves of your loved ones. I will mourn with you the loss of friends. I will cry your tears. I will take your judgments. I will never leave you. I will love you even when you hate me. Even when "I am despised and rejected by men", I will never despise or reject you.'

Jesus reinvents our God for us, presenting him back to us: 'his image in our flesh'. To see him, we must dare ourselves to unlearn what we have learnt. The One whom Israel expected failed to materialise. The salvation and deliverance that they prayed for was answered in a way that was unrecognisable. Nazareth missed it, but when we see their story, we can see the glorious truth.

Marvel now at the picture that Jesus is painting! He embraces the illegitimate because he knows their reproach. He embraces the outcast because he knows their pain. He embraces the child in us who has been misunderstood, bullied, provoked, isolated, lied about, dealt with and cast aside. He knows the damning isolation because he was damned and isolated. He became that child.

And as we see this Jesus, so we see God. The God who declares:

> Surely He has borne our griefs
> And carried our sorrows . . .
> For thus says the High and Lofty One
> Who inhabits eternity, whose name is Holy:
> 'I dwell in the high and holy place,
> With him who has a contrite and humble spirit,
> To revive the spirit of the humble,
> And to revive the spirit of the contrite ones.'

God has descended from the glory of eternity to live the life of an illegitimate child in a town stricken with shame concerning its fallen daughter. Mary broke the heart of her village, failing to meet every expectation that her family had for her—yet all the while fulfilling God's every expectation! God came to live the life of Mary's son so that every orphan, every illegitimate, every unwed mother, every betrayed father—every one of us who hides our 'sicknesses' under tightly wound bandages—has the hope and comfort that he 'knows' because he 'lived'.

Now the downcast, the outcast, the marginalised can hear the words:

> Arise, shine;
> For your light has come!
> And the glory of the Lord has risen upon *you*.

This is God to us.

Let the glory of this rise on us as the impact of Nazareth redefines God for us. Let us leave the safety of what we know and walk the streets looking for 'Mary and Jesus'. Let us look for the God who came to live in Nazareth. Can we re-examine our lives with their rights and wrongs, their beliefs and judgments? Can we stand in our 'synagogues', listening to the 'words about God' among those who believe and judge with us, and look for Mary and Jesus? Do we have the courage to 'see' him? Are we able to free ourselves from protecting and defending all we believe so that we can live our lives with Jesus? Will we swim against the tide in our 'Nazareth' or join the crowd in their shortsighted wisdom and judgment?

Our Nazareth is white, prosperous, middle-class and Western, while Jesus is more like the poor, the coloured, the black and the marginalised. Our Nazareth is legitimate and still struggles with the illegitimacy that Jesus embraced. Our Nazareth is judging the 'headline' of the unwed mother while her child has to live in her 'story'. Are we prepared to see that Jesus embraced the story of this little child, or do we take both of them to our cliff face?

Our Nazareth needs to make 'headline judgments' so that we can rid ourselves of the accountability, identification and empathy demanded by the 'stories'. The headlines scream out for justice. The stories cry out for mercy. The headlines form an angry crowd. The stories are lived alone. We can become part of the 'shock-jock herd', besieging the airwaves with our intolerant, self-righteous indignation, or we can be compassionately joined to the stories. We have the choice. Do we live on the side of those who are judged on the cliff face, or do we form lynch mobs in our 'synagogues', wherever they may be?

Are we courageous enough to admit that we just might find Jesus in a cell in Darwin, pleading with a fellow victim of abused justice as a nation refuses to have a heart? Can we hear his empathetic words as an Aboriginal youth comes to the end of his ability to see any hope in his future? If Jesus can stand before the judgmental hearts of Nazareth and announce unconditional salvation, can't we find the same grace in ourselves? How can we attend our Sunday services, eating his flesh and drinking his blood, shaking hands with our constituents and kissing babies, while the young men and women of our nation still suffer under our 'justice'? How can we justify our self-righteousness?

If Jesus can come to our Nazareth, we must go with him to the 'legal injecting rooms' and the back streets of Kings Cross (so accurately named). We must go with him to the outskirts of Australian country towns, to the squalor of the settlements that we pretend don't exist. We must go because he is already there. Can we allow a chink in our moral armour long enough to let the light in for those who are lost in darkness? If we refuse the light, what do we expect to happen to the dark?

What is our choice? Do we join Nazareth? Or do we join Jesus?

What would we do, White Australia, if God chose Mount Isa's daughter, Mary, and named her first black offspring Jesus? What would we do, Immigrant Australia, those of us who have left our lands in whatever generation to arrive here as uninvited guests, if Mary was a fisherman's daughter on the banks of the Parramatta River in 1737, thirty-three years before Captain Cook 'took possession' of the country for King George III?

What would you do if Mary was your daughter? Would you see Jesus in her illegitimate child? Or would you comfort yourself with your standards at the cliff face?

We must choose every day. When we chose to accept Jesus' claims, then all that is sad and fallen about our Nazareth compels us to bring his message of identification and compassion.

The question has to be 'will the real God please stand up?' Is he the God that every Nazareth expects, or the God of Jesus Christ that every Nazareth rejects? The God who fulfils our expectations, or the God who comes according to his own?

These are tough questions. But if we don't answer them, we remain in Nazareth and Nazareth remains in us.

Jesus had to start in Nazareth before he could go to Galilee. He had to bring the glorious truth to light by making it flesh. As Jesus walked away from the cliff top of small town bigotry, he didn't wash his hands. He didn't sentence Nazareth to judgment. He took his pain, rejection and identification and, presenting Nazareth as his credential, walked the dusty roads of earth looking into the eyes of those who lived under the same curse of self-righteous judgment.

Thirty years in Nazareth were a wonderful visitation that will forever bring hope to all who feel the reproach of Joseph, Mary and their family. This is what Jesus was offering that day in the synagogue. He opened the door to a kingdom of God that admits those who are rejected by every other kingdom, that accepts those who can admit the failure that is the reason for their exclusion. It is a kingdom that begins to rejoice as Jesus is revealed standing outside our expectations, standing with the ones who are judged as unworthy. It is a kingdom that makes us responsible for all we have done and said as we live, blinded by our own prejudice, in Nazareth. When this kingdom comes to us, his will can be done through us, 'on earth as it is in heaven'.

Jesus opened the door to a kingdom that admits those rejected by every other kingdom.

What was dead to Nazareth can be alive to us.

Do we want to continue to throw stones from the cliff face? Or will we join Jesus and heal those whom we have wounded? When we recognise Mary's son, we must change the way we live in Nazareth.

Jesus has come. Can we see him? Or are the disappointments of Nazareth still in the way?

6

*C*ana

'Sing, O barren,
You who have not borne!
Break forth into singing and cry aloud,
You who have not laboured with child!
For more are the children of the desolate
Than the children of the married woman,' says the Lord . . .
Do not fear, for you will not be ashamed;
Neither be disgraced, for you will not be put to shame;
For you will forget the shame of your youth,
And will not remember the reproach of your widowhood anymore.
For your Maker is your husband,
The Lord of hosts is His name;
And your Redeemer is the Holy One of Israel;
He is called the God of the whole earth . . .
Ho! Everyone who thirsts,
Come to the waters;
And you who have no money,
Come, buy and eat.
Yes, come, buy wine and milk
Without money and without price.
Why do you spend money for what is not bread,
And your wages for what does not satisfy?
Listen carefully to Me, and eat what is good,
And let your soul delight itself in abundance.
Incline your ear, and come to Me.
Hear and your soul shall live.

Jesus finally made his public entrance onto the stage of history by travelling from Nazareth to the Jordan River where John the Baptist was performing his ministry. It was here that he was baptised. John took one look at him and exclaimed that he was not worthy to perform the event, but he relented when Jesus told him that he must 'for thus it is fitting for us to fulfil all righteousness'.

> When He had been baptised, Jesus came up immediately from the water; and behold, the heavens were opened to Him, and He saw the Spirit of God descending like a dove and alighting upon Him. And suddenly a voice came from heaven, saying, 'This is My beloved Son, in whom I am well pleased.'

Later John saw Jesus and exclaimed, 'Behold the Lamb of God!' Some of John's disciples were within earshot, and one of them was Andrew, Simon Peter's brother. Andrew found Simon and took him to Jesus, who looked at Simon and said, 'You are Simon the son of Jonah. You shall be called Cephas.' 'Cephas' means 'a stone'. There and then Simon Peter started a journey that would change his life. Many times his thoughts would return to this simple scene as he heard for the first time the voice of Jesus.

Another disciple was Philip. He was from the same home town as Andrew and Simon Peter, Bethsaida. Philip also heard those wonderful but rather strange words that changed every life they were addressed to: 'Follow me.'

Having gathered a small band of disciples, Jesus then left and took them to, of all places, a wedding.

John tells us that Jesus' mother was there and that Jesus and his disciples were invited. No doubt they knew the bride and groom's families—Cana was not far from Nazareth. But it was a long way from the Jordan River in Judea to Galilee. Jesus and his band had to travel north from the Jordan Valley, past Capernaum, up through the Megiddo Valley and into the hills to Cana. Quite a trek! What was so important about this wedding that they made such a journey? What were they about to learn that required a 'retreat' in the country?

Jewish weddings are not little ceremonies followed by afternoon tea, poor speeches, some gushing from ancient aunts, stilted photos, more gushing, tearful tipsy goodbyes, confetti, and then a race to the airport to catch the 'Great Barrier Reef Honeymoon Flight'. Jewish weddings involved the whole village and went for days. The bride's family honoured the groom's family with the lavishness of the celebrations. The whole community gathered to celebrate, and the entire event was seen as a crucial foundation for the newlyweds' future. Honour was at stake. Both families' names were at stake. The relationship between the new in-laws was on the line. One father's daughter was being given away with a sizeable dowry, and another father, his son and his family were receiving the respect that such occasions demanded.

It was a very important social, cultural and religious event. It was expensive, lavish and everything hinged on its success.

And when they ran out of wine . . .

These seven words are often missed while we rush on impatiently to make sense of this controversial miracle. But they are crucial for understanding Jesus' actions. It was for these seven words that Jesus brought his disciples to Cana.

I have been to countless weddings. I have played piano as many brides have walked down the aisle. I am prone to uncontrolled emotions, and I cannot tell you the number of brides I have 'cried' for as they have made their journey towards the minister. Even complete strangers! Sometimes the 'mother of the bride' looks at me quizzically as I try to sniffle in time to the music, comforting myself with the knowledge that the groom and his football team mates are looking in the other direction. I have listened to couples make a complete mess of their vows, ministers make a complete mess of their readings, and soloists make a complete mess of me. I remember many clerics who have omitted large parts of the service because of nerves. I know one who had to meet the newlyweds after their honeymoon so they could complete the signing of the register and he could finally, legally declare them husband and wife—three weeks late!

I have waited for brides to arrive over an hour late. I have watched as bridesmaids, groomsmen, brides and grooms have fainted, collapsed, forgotten rings, lost shoes, ripped dresses, tripped, not turned up and almost thrown up.

After the ceremony comes the reception, marked by good food, old food, stale food, cold food, no food, little wine, no wine (not unusual at all), too much wine, bad wine (often), long speeches, longer speeches, bad speeches, angry speeches, bad jokes, rude jokes, obscene jokes, happy brides, sad brides, drunk brides . . . In the end, the confused and exhausted couple are tossed into the back of some car; they wave and we wave; they go and we go. End of story—until the slide night after the honeymoon, if you ever get the chance to see the happy pair again.

Although Australian weddings are momentous occasions, when Aussie girls and Aussie blokes get carried away pretending to be someone they're not, all that usually happens is that bad taste triumphs over good taste and everyone has a giggle or ten. Not much damage is done.

In Cana, however, they were facing a disaster of truly 'biblical' proportions!

They had run out of wine. The bride's father had either failed to buy enough or the town of Cana had drunk excessively. Whatever the cause and the state of the guests, the real issue was not the wine. The real issue concerned the young couple, newly married, with their whole lives stretching out before them.

Running out of wine was not a catering problem. It was a matter of honour. If the bride or groom found out—or even worse, the family of the groom—it would be such an insult, such a humiliation, that everything concerning their union would be tainted forever.

What was at stake here was a matter of 'blessing or cursing'. The rest of their lives was about to be 'cursed' by events that were beyond their control. Their children, their extended family, all that would ever concern them and be remembered about them, would be impacted by this disaster. More than that, there was no answer. No solution. The sentence was sure and the consequences would be swift and long-lasting.

Running out of wine was not a catering problem. It was a matter of honour.

This was a pivotal point in the history of the bride's family. They were about to be thrown onto the mercy of the groom's father, and he was about to be insulted in front of the whole village.

Mary came to Jesus. She had seen what had happened and she knew—oh, so personally—what would happen as a result. She said to Jesus, 'They have no wine!' It was not a simple statement of fact but a forlorn cry from the depths of a broken heart.

Why would Jesus bother to do anything? For years I just couldn't understand it, especially when John writes: 'This beginning of signs Jesus did in Cana of Galilee, and manifested His glory; and His disciples believed in Him.' Why would this miracle be the first, and how did it manifest his glory? Surely there were greater miracles that would announce Christ to the world. Surely every miracle that came after this wedding would have been more appropriate.

But Jesus, with the foresight that had its foundation in eternity, planned for this miracle to define every other. What we must see, therefore, is not *what* he did, but *why*.

It may sound improbable, but the meaning came to me while I was on a bus in, of all places, Cana.

We had just visited Nazareth, and my mind was still spinning from my tour guide's words, 'When Jesus lived here, this was a small village of about twelve families.' As we wound our way along the narrow roads past all the tourist spots, I was reflecting on how much difference the reality of Jesus' Nazareth made to my understanding of him. Jesus had not come to Jerusalem, though that would have made much more sense, and he had not come to Rome, though that would have been ideal, at least by human standards. No, he had come to a tiny village to live a life that would forever bring comfort to all.

As we rumbled into Cana I thought of the same small town mentality. Here Jesus encountered the same injustice as Nazareth, as culture and tradition were about to combine with misinterpreted actions, unintended insults and irreversible reactions. Cana was about to turn a celebration into an insult that would forever sentence these 'innocents' to a cursed future.

Do you ever find it amazing that Jesus doesn't simply point out the abuse that lies in our culture? He comes into our lives and respects the demands of our culture, even when these demands are so unjust. We should learn a lesson here. Jesus comes to the individual and brings hope, no matter what the circumstances.

This is the glory of God. It is not about the miracles. They are symptoms of the heart of God as he breaks out of eternity and enters human frailty, life and death. The glory of God is seen in the most glorious revelation of all—that God 'knows' because he 'lived'. Jesus knew the pain of this couple. He knew it because he knew *them*. He knew their families.

> **Jesus came to reveal the heart of God to those who were expecting God to be somebody else.**

He knew their reactions. And even more precious—more precious than the supernatural that was about to bring about their rescue, more precious than any other thing that I can dare to imagine God doing or saying—Jesus knew the pain that the situation would cause them because he had lived that pain.

This is the God who has come to us. This is his glory.

Why oh why have we missed this, arguing instead about alcohol? This story is not about the immorality of excess; it is about the immorality of judgment.

This couple were about to be judged as a consequence of actions. 'Headlines.' Every time we look at this story we do exactly the same thing as we try to determine what Jesus was saying about the 'headline' of alcohol. We miss his lesson entirely. *In Cana, Jesus simply takes the curse of impending judgment and fashions it into a gift of new life.* When we miss this, we continue in our judgments, denying the new life, the new start, that Jesus is pleading be extended through us.

Jesus came to reveal the heart of God, the character of God, the very identity of God to those who were expecting God to be somebody else. Jesus came to join himself to our story, choosing not to join the others in judging the headlines. Perhaps he looked at the innocent face of the bride basking in the beauty and love of this, her day. Perhaps he caught the confident expression of the bridegroom as he, unaware of the calamity that had befallen them, planned his future, naming his sons. Whatever he saw, he felt it deep inside his human heart. A heart that beat inside a simple carpenter's son, rejected by his village because he didn't fulfil the requirements of their moral codes.

He says to his mother: 'Woman, what does your concern have

to do with me? My hour has not yet come.' Then perhaps he looked into her eyes and realised that this had everything to do with him.

Behind those eyes, buried deep inside Mary's broken heart, was the memory of another wedding day. What were her feelings as she walked with her family to Cana? She was now a widow. She had no husband by her side. What 'photographs' adorned Mary's mantelpiece? Was there a framed and faded hand-coloured print of a young Mary in a once-worn bridal gown, standing nervous and excited beside her young Joseph? Did she have the memories of her wedding to comfort her in old age? No. All Mary had was the hurried cover-up, the cancelled plans and the shame of a village that forced itself not to throw stones.

Jesus looked into his mother's life and knew that *his* story was the cause of her pain. Yes, her pain revealed Jesus in such a way that humankind would have to think twice before they chose to judge. But she was so innocent and faithful—a teenage girl who grew up with the voice of an angel ringing in her ears as every other voice condemned her. Perhaps Jesus looked from his mother to the young couple drinking from their special goblets and thought ahead to the judgment that Cana was about to inflict on them. It was all so unjust.

But there was nothing Jesus could do. He knew their pain—knew it first-hand—and he saw it in his mother, her eyes imploring him, searching his eyes for the answer that she had longed thirty years for. But he could do nothing because his time had not yet come.

His time had not come when his family was reviled and shunned by the village. His time had not come when he discovered the death of his father. His time had not come when Nazareth tried to throw him off the cliff. Time and time again he had wished that he could explain all the pain he was causing his loved ones—that he could shine his glory for an instant, secretly, so that they would know the truth. But no, he had to wait for his Father. Jesus' hands were tied. He made it constantly clear that he and his Father were one. He could do nothing apart from his Father, and therefore they were all still waiting.

Then all of a sudden, there in Cana at a wedding feast, the most miraculous thing happened. In between one verse and the next in the book of John is an unwritten conversation that must have taken place before this miracle could be done. Jesus must have known that there would come a day when his Father would say, 'Now.' All through his life Jesus had waited, longing, his heart reaching out yet restrained. Now he looked at his mother with her broken heart and at these two young people whose lives were about to be shattered by pettiness, and he heard the words:

'Jesus, my Son, now is the time!'

There can be no other explanation.

> Arise, shine, Cana . . .
> Arise, shine, Galilee . . .
> Arise, shine, Israel, holy land by the Mediterranean Sea, on this little planet, in this insignificant solar system, orbiting a tiny sun.
> Arise, shine; for your light has come! And the glory of the Lord has risen upon you.

Where and when did this wonderful prophecy of Isaiah come to pass, the angels and elders ask God in eternity.

In a little village at a wedding.

For all human history past, human beings have been 'coming to God'. But now we have a God who comes to us, to a family wedding, to declare his glory.

Everything about God has changed.

'His time had come.'

I wonder how Jesus felt during those seconds as time stood still and all eternity stooped to see? What did he think? Did he look at his mother and smile? Was there suddenly the reassurance in his eyes that she had longed for? Did he draw a deep breath as he realised that the clock had finally started and every moment would now bring him closer to the climax of his mission?

Jesus called to the servants, telling them to go and fill six stone water pots to the brim with water.

What did Mary think? For the first time, Jesus was moving beyond the stubborn barrier that had continually made her wait for the fulfilment of the angel's words all those years ago. How she had longed for this moment. She had imagined miracles, power, glory, marvels . . .

And now her son was simply making wine.

This was his hour? This?

Did Mary see the significance of the moment? Did she understand the glory that was about to be revealed? Or had she, too, been caught up in the expectations that she had for her son Jesus?

She said to the servants, 'Whatever he says to you, do it.' And she watched as they filled the six stone water pots.

These water pots were used for ritual washing and purification. They were large—very large. They contained, when full, between 90 and 135 litres each. And they were now full.

And He said to them, 'Draw some out now, and take it to the master of the feast.' And they took it. When the master of the feast tasted the water that was made wine, and did not know where it came from . . . the master of the feast called the bridegroom. And he said to him, 'Every man at the beginning sets out the good wine, and when the guests have well drunk, then the inferior. You have kept the good wine until now!'

Jesus turned this young couple's dying dream into a celebratory toast with the best wine of the feast! What was lost to them was now found for them.

'His time had come.'

Jesus had made between 540 and 810 litres of wine. Great wine. The best wine. There was no possible way the guests could drink it all, so Jesus had not only turned disaster into celebration but provided a sizeable 'dowry' for the couple's future. The wine was now a considerable asset. Jesus had reversed their fortunes.

Forgiveness is not just a clean slate and the freedom to start again. Forgiveness is salvation. When life has come to an end and the way is barred, Jesus offers us his life in exchange for ours. This is an overwhelming gift that is both unexpected and undeserved. Our bankruptcy is transformed into the kingdom of heaven.

No wonder it is called 'new wine'!

> This beginning of signs Jesus did in Cana of Galilee, and manifested His glory; and His disciples believed in Him.

Did his disciples really understand what had taken place, or were they simply impressed by the supernatural? I wonder if they too stumbled over the excessive amounts of alcohol involved. Perhaps they discussed this on the way home. Could they have wanted to exert influence on this strange miracle worker? Perhaps they wished he had not been so generous. Perhaps they wished he had turned the water into strong coffee. No one would stumble over strong coffee.

Here at the beginning of Jesus' ministry, we see the first indications of what would later become so clear. The people of Galilee would start to follow Jesus the miracle worker. They were looking for signs. But they failed to see the greatest sign of all. This sign, written in Nazareth and now revealed in Cana, was about to shine brighter and brighter. There was so much more to come. Jesus would be glorified again and again. His glory, however, came not in the fulfilment of a nation's desires for the Messiah they longed for. His glory was revealed every time he stood aside from their expectations and hopes, refusing to fit the image they set before him. Whenever Jesus was moved with compassion, the greatest miracle was that this compassion had come so far to touch, to hold, to embrace and to heal.

Jesus stepped over cultural barriers. He ignored religious boundaries, moral codes and social traditions.

This compassion was expressed to all. Jesus stepped over cultural barriers. He ignored religious boundaries, moral codes and social traditions. He was continually found where no Messiah would be sought. For all who had felt the judgment and rejection of these boundaries, this was so glorious.

And it still is. The glory that God brings to the marginalised makes *all* our expectations of glory pale into insignificance. When we fail to see the opportunity to offer Jesus' gift of new life to others, preferring instead to judge the morality of the circumstances, we miss the glory of Cana, and we miss the glory of God. We are left with the same petty squabbles that haunted every step Jesus made. Yes, he still worked miracles while the Pharisees bickered on the sidelines, but it was they who were the poorer. They missed the glory of God. They chose their own idea of glory instead. They continued to study by the light of their own lamps, shortsightedly looking up from their books to see whether the world and its Creator were still conforming to the little that they knew and the less that they sought.

The followers of Jesus marvelled at his works of power, and of course the miracles were marvellous (and still are, especially when you are on the receiving end!). But it is when we look from the miracles to Jesus that we see the truly miraculous.

It is not *what* he did that proclaimed his kingdom, it is *why* he did it.

When we look at the miracle of God in the flesh of Jesus, the miracles of healing are not diminished. They simply become wonderful examples of a far greater truth.

This is the glory of Cana.

7

Capernaum

The Spirit of the Lord God is upon Me,
Because the Lord has anointed Me
To preach good tidings to the poor;
He has sent Me to heal the brokenhearted,
To proclaim liberty to the captives,
And the opening of the prison to those who are bound;
To proclaim the acceptable year of the Lord,
And the day of vengeance of our God;
To comfort all who mourn,
To console those who mourn in Zion,
To give them beauty for ashes,
The oil of joy for mourning,
The garment of praise for the spirit of heaviness;
That they may be called trees of righteousness,
The planting of the Lord, that He may be glorified.

At the time of writing, the United States of America is going through the processes that will result in the election of their next President. Every night our news is full of the machinations of the various candidates as they throw mud at each other. Behind each candidate is an office full of 'spin doctors'. These advisers specialise in making 'bad news' into 'good news' by putting a 'spin' on its interpretation. The recent history of the Presidency is full of such examples, but so is every government and every politician's filing cabinet.

'Welfare cuts', for example, can be explained without the 'spin', like this: 'The government has decided to cut its welfare budget. This will profoundly affect low income earners and pensioners. The government is doing this to provide tax cuts for high income earners. This will greatly enhance the government's chances of re-election. It will also fund the unfulfilled promises from the last election.'

Now let's put a 'spin' on the story: 'Today the government is announcing a broad new initiative that will lighten the tax burden on Australian families. This "new tax initiative" will provide greater resources for the economy. It will release funds into the building industry, the banking sector and the retail sector. It will also provide much needed support for non-government welfare organisations. The Prime Minister is encouraging all businesses to act responsibly in sharing the "welfare load". The government has also set up a "Welfare Task Force" to provide help and advice to those in need.'

Sound familiar?

The 'spin doctors' also have to deal with a candidate's or politician's past (not to mention the present and future if their charge 'puts his foot in it'!). The 'good news' is broadcast to millions: the military service and the medals, the courage under fire, the great leadership abilities and so on. Other parts of their charge's life are overlooked or re-explained. There is a classic 'spin' about inhaling that illustrates my point.

Almost every 'office' that bears any popular influence needs 'spin'. Even Shane Warne needs 'spin' these days!

It seems that after the events in Cana Jesus decided to move from Nazareth to Capernaum on the Sea of Galilee. When he arrived he started to preach. Some of his companions apparently went back to their trade, because one day Jesus was walking along the shore and noticed Simon and Andrew casting their nets into the sea. They were doing what their family had done for generations. He called to them, 'Follow Me, and I will make you fishers of men,' and they downed tools and immediately followed him.

Jesus then walked a little further and called out to two other brothers, James and John. These two were in the family boat with their father, Zebedee, mending nets. Now I am sure that this was not as much fun as fishing. I have seen many fishermen practising 'catching nothing' and I have seen the equipment that helps them 'catch nothing'. Every one of these eager fishermen works in a state of high motivation. Though I have never seen them mending their nets with much enthusiasm, they still do it, because mending nets is all about fishing. You don't mend nets unless you are serious about using them.

Mending nets may be boring, but walking away from the family business is extraordinary.

So James and John were mending nets because they were committed to their fishing. Yet Jesus called to them and they immediately stopped what they were doing, left their poor old dad behind and followed him.

Mending nets may be boring, but walking away from the shared responsibility of the family business is extraordinary. Two sons leave their father and put an enormous strain on their family relationships. In the account in the Gospel of Mark, we're told that the Zebedee family also had a number of hired servants who were helping. John and James were part of a family enterprise that required wages to be paid. In the account in Luke, we find that the brothers were actually in partnership with Simon and Andrew. Simon, Andrew, James, John, Zebedee, hired servants and perhaps other families—all in business together. This was no isolated stroll beside the lake where some lads were fishing, telling tall tales of the one that got away and deciding to become 'fishers of men' because there was nothing better to do for the afternoon! No, this was a family upheaval.

Relationships would have been tested to the core. Finances would have been stretched to the limit. New helpers would have to be hired—and all of Capernaum would have known!

Simon, Andrew, James and John already knew Jesus and been exposed to his teaching. Perhaps you are thinking they followed because they were extraordinarily gifted with 'spiritual insight', but if this was the case, it was the first and last time they ever exhibited it. The rest of the Gospels and a good part of the book of Acts deal with their complete lack of spiritual insight. After all, how many times did God have to beat Peter over the head with a vision in Joppa before he finally relented and went to the house of Cornelius?

> And leaving Nazareth, He came and dwelt in Capernaum, which is by the sea... From that time Jesus began to preach and to say, 'Repent, for the kingdom of heaven is at hand.'

Capernaum was a large town. It contained a Roman garrison and a synagogue. Capernaum became the Galilean headquarters for Jesus and his band of followers. They would have been front page news. Look at the story so far and what we have already discussed concerning Nazareth and Cana. Combine it with what we now see in this town and place it in the mouths of the incredulous family and friends of these four middle-class professional fishermen. You can almost hear the conversations that night:

'Hey, have you heard about Zebedee? His business is on the skids. His boys and their two mates have left the partnership and have taken up with that teacher from Nazareth. I have friends in Nazareth. Have you been there? You have to look pretty hard to find it. You should hear what they say about him! Who does he think he is? He got thrown out of home, turned the place upside down, insulted the synagogue ruler by teaching heresy in the synagogue, and then he comes here. And what does he do? He wrecks one of the best businesses in town!'

Even some of the friends of Jesus' disciples had questions. In John 1, for example, after Jesus called Philip to follow him, Philip found Nathanael and said, 'We have found Him of whom Moses in the law, and also the prophets, wrote—Jesus of Nazareth, the son of Joseph.' But Nathaniel replied, 'Can anything good come out of Nazareth?'

You don't have to use a great deal of imagination once you put the whole story together. *We* know who Jesus is, but we have some pretty powerful proof. They didn't. They were expecting the Messiah, but at the moment Jesus was doing some very un-Messiah-like things.

It would be easy to believe that Jesus came and floated above the ground, creating an atmosphere of faith wherever he went. It would be easy to believe that this Christ was believed in by his family, his friends, his neighbours in Nazareth and now his neighbours in his new home in Capernaum. It would be easy to have a fairy tale gospel where everyone lives happily ever after. But we know the truth about the ending. If the ending is so dark, then we'd better look at the story again.

What was it that Jesus did that constantly divided all who heard of him?

> And Jesus went about all Galilee, teaching in their synagogues, preaching the gospel of the kingdom, and healing all kinds of sickness and all kinds of disease among the people. Then His fame went throughout all Syria; and they brought to Him all sick people who were afflicted with various diseases and torments, and those who were demon-possessed, epileptics, and paralytics; and He healed them. Great multitudes followed Him . . .

Jesus didn't fit the expectations. He didn't have a 'spin' on his ministry. He refused to water anything down as he went about his work. This would have infuriated all who followed him, especially the 'spin doctors'. (If you look at the statements that Peter made throughout the rest of his life, you will discover a consummate 'spin doctor'. Even the apostle Paul had to bring him into line.) Just when the crowds were in awe and the hush had settled on the thousands witnessing the supernatural—just when the 'kingdom' that all were expecting seemed imminent—Jesus would do something crazy and the wheels would fall off their revolutionary cart. To everyone who followed him, this 'kingdom' would have been their greatest expectation, but their interpretations of it were as varied as the followers themselves. In the end, although the miracles flowed from his hands, many were disappointed because he would not answer *their* prayers, fulfil *their* hopes or build *their* kingdom.

Look at Capernaum.

If you travel to Galilee today you can find the ruins of Capernaum. They are by the lake, about thirty minutes drive from Tiberias. In the middle of the ruins are two holy sites. One is the ruins of a house that is said to have belonged to Peter. The other is the ruins of the synagogue that was built on the rubble of the earlier synagogue of Jesus' time. You can walk up the steps and look across the lake to the hills of the Golan Heights. Jesus stood on this spot and turned the town upside down.

Jesus called the disciples by the lake and then a few days later went to the synagogue. Here he cast a demon out of a man who kept interjecting throughout his message. He then went to Simon's house, which was two streets across from the synagogue. Here he healed the mother of Simon's wife. (It is interesting to note that this is the only time Simon Peter's wife is mentioned.) By the end of the day, the whole city had gathered at the door. Jesus 'healed many who were sick with various diseases, and cast out many demons; and He did not allow the demons to speak, because they knew Him.'

Over the next few days the momentum built. News spreads

fast. Everyone was excited. Multitudes gathered at Simon Peter's house. Then Jesus healed a leper . . . and now the scribes and Pharisees were sent to observe.

The scribes and Pharisees. I can almost hear the audience hiss and boo.

But this is not a melodramatic fairy tale. This is life in Galilee. This is humanity going about its business, trying to understand, trying to know, trying to get ahead, and appointing those who have the knowledge and wisdom to lead the way. The scribes and Pharisees were trusted with this community responsibility, and they were well respected for it.

Imagine you are with the four brothers, Simon, Andrew, James and John. You have known these guys and their families for years. They are fishermen. Their families own two boats and they are quite successful. They are well-known about town. But so much has happened in their lives over the last few days and weeks.

> **The scribes and Pharisees. I can almost hear the audience hiss and boo.**

They have thrown everything away to follow this Jesus. They believe he may be the Messiah. Unbelievable!

They are very excited, in spite of everything being said about them. And you share their enthusiasm. After all, if they have made such a momentous decision, there must be something to this Nazarene. And admit it, this is much better than fishing! The last few days since they returned from Cana have been extraordinary, and your head is spinning. Your imagination runs riot as you daydream of the kingdom that has been the conversation point at every meal in every town since the exiles returned from Babylon. You can't help yourself. You look at the Roman centurions leaning on their spears, watching the crowds, listening to the exclamations, and you think of King David. You think of his victories and of the might and splendour of his kingdom. And you too dare to believe that this one, this Jesus from Nazareth of all places, may be the 'Son of David'.

You nudge the others in the ribs and point to the scribes and Pharisees as they conspicuously make their way to Simon's house. The crowds part for them and there is anticipation in the air. These men will tell you the truth. They know who the Messiah should be. One look at Jesus and they will pronounce him 'Him of whom Moses in the law and also the prophets wrote'. After all, these men *know* the law and the prophets. The crowd almost sings with excitement.

You secretly say a prayer for Jesus, praying for favour, praying that the scribes and Pharisees will be impressed. You wish that you could get closer to speak to him. You could offer some advice; you know these men well. And you pray again for a great sign, a miracle.

Then you glance again towards your four friends, the fishermen. You catch something in their expressions that puzzles you. They seem to know something, and it seems to be bothering them. Maybe something happened in Cana. However, too much is happening here in Capernaum, and you dismiss it for now.

The next few hours are not what you expect, and frankly you wish they hadn't happened at all. Yes, there was a great miracle—the greatest one so far, in fact. But Jesus didn't play his part so well. The others are not happy either, and much is being said across the town. Sure, it was only a little thing, but 'little things' can become large obstructions where the law is concerned. And thanks to what happened, this new ministry suddenly has a huge boulder in its path. It was the last thing that Jesus, Simon, Andrew, James and John needed. What they really needed was a blessing from the scribes and Pharisees. Now, to be blunt, the scribes and Pharisees had pronounced the opposite.

They were in the house. Jesus was teaching. The scribes and Pharisees were seated near the front, for it was thought that this would be a 'plus'. Suddenly, dust and leaves started to fall from the roof—a little at first and then in great chunks. They fell on Jesus' head and the heads of those nearest him. Naturally everyone looked up, even the Pharisees. Someone was on the roof. They were removing the tiles. Faces appeared, and before much could be said, the hole was made so large that the sun streamed in. So much for the roof! Then, just when everyone thought they had seen everything, a man on a bed was lowered through the roof by four other men. He hovered in mid-air until he came to rest in front of Jesus. The man was crippled.

All eyes turned from the roof to the man on the bed, to the dumbstruck Pharisees and finally to Jesus. What now?

It didn't take long. It happened so quickly, but it changed everything.

> When He saw their faith, He said to him, 'Man, your sins are forgiven you.' And the scribes and the Pharisees began to reason, saying, 'Who is this who speaks blasphemies? Who can forgive sins but God alone?'

Good question.

> But when Jesus perceived their thoughts, He answered and said to them, 'Why are you reasoning in your hearts? Which is easier, to say, "Your sins are forgiven you," or to say, "Rise up and walk"? But that you may know that the Son of Man has power on earth to forgive sins'—He said to the man who was paralysed, 'I say to you, arise, take up your bed, and go to your house.'

The man stood up, took his bedding and went home. And he was not quiet about it. As he walked out you could hear his friends sliding off the roof, shouting their heads off.

The scribes and Pharisees were not impressed. They didn't even notice the healing. They noticed the blasphemy. Everyone did.

If what Jesus said was true, then he was the Messiah. But if it wasn't true, then the man was still unpardoned and the miracle was wrought by some other 'power'.

Surely the evidence of the miracle speaks for itself! Or does it? This is very troubling.

It would have been wonderful to stop here before all hell broke loose, but it was far too late. After a shaky start in his home town, and after creating turmoil at the waterfront, Jesus' ministry got underway with an awesome display of the miraculous. His words of compassion became works of compassion. He healed. He delivered. He forgave and pardoned. The kingdom had come, and whatever was said about his past faded as each day dawned with a greater hope.

Jesus, however, had declared war. He had disqualified himself as the Messiah of the scribes and Pharisees. There was now division, and this division would grow into a chasm. No one could stop talking about what he said to the paralytic. It was the greatest topic of the day. It was debated across Capernaum.

The man and his sickness may been forgotten in the midst of the controversy. Controversy often disconnects our hearts as we try to use our heads. But Jesus had entered this man's story. His healing was not simply about the paralysis of his body. It went far deeper than that.

Look again and see what we so often miss. The poor man was paralysed. His whole life was at the mercy of others. The climate of faith at that time presented him with the horrid distortion that his sickness resulted from God's judgment. Consequently he was paralysed in soul and spirit as well as body. Every day he lay under the judgment of God. His body was simply the evidence of God's displeasure.

Imagine what he felt when he heard that this Jesus of Nazareth may be the Messiah. Was he excited that God had come to his home town of Capernaum? Or was he stricken with the fear that God had come to judge his sins personally? His friends came and told him the most wonderful things about this Jesus, but his heart could not receive it. Why? Because his God had sentenced him to this stretcher. His God was angry and demanded more of him than he could give. He had tried everything and everything was not enough. Obviously God knew something that he didn't, and it was this 'secret sin' that had sentenced his life to such horrid rejection. He feared this God.

It was easy to get excited when you hadn't fallen into God's hands. His friends were lucky—'blessed' with the favour of good health. He was not blessed. He was cursed. If the Messiah had turned up, his worst fear had arrived.

His friends grabbed his stretcher. There was nothing he could do to stop them. They carried him into town, past the condescending stares of the marketplace, past the synagogue, through the milling crowds to Simon Peter's house. What were they doing? Suddenly he was hoisted above the heads of the crowd, and before he knew it he was on the roof. He was absolutely humiliated—and worse was yet to come. His friends hatched a plan. They made a large hole by removing the tiles. He was going to be lowered through this hole, alone, to arrive guilty, judged and paralysed at the feet of Jesus. He was beyond himself with fear and he was powerless to stop them.

He was at their mercy, and soon he would be at the mercy of the Messiah.

Why were his friends doing this?

Perhaps it was simply because they wanted him to find out what he needed to do about the secret sin that must have caused God's judgment to fall on his stricken body. Perhaps Jesus would be able to tell their sick friend why this had happened, and what he should do so that God would lift the sentence of judgment.

But the poor man was in misery. His dark secret sins were about to be told to a house full of religious zealots, sins that are so great they had brought this horrible judgment on him. What on earth would God require from him to atone for whatever it was he had done? What sacrifice could he possibly afford? How would he present it?

It took an eternity to travel through the air above the heads of the crowd.

His eyes were clenched shut. He heard laughter and some poor jokes at his expense. He hit the floor with a jolt.

Silence.

He opened his eyes and looked into the face of God.

Jesus looked through this poor wretch's sickness and saw a heart that had been riddled with blasphemous lies. Jesus' first words to the cripple were the last ones the man thought he would ever hear. His guilt plagued his every thought. His guilt silenced all hope.

Jesus said, 'Man, your sins are forgiven you.'

Can you think of anything more wonderful? God came and stepped out of the fearful expectations of this poor paralytic and redefined himself in his paralysed spirit. What had barred his heart from ever hoping was now overwhelmingly overcome.

God came to forgive what this man could never forgive in himself. Why? Because his body lied to him. His spiritual community lied to him. He wouldn't have been able to accept forgiveness unless it came in the place of impending judgment. Just as depression sentences all its victims to a life devoid of happiness and hope, often without obvious cause, so too this man's guilt sentenced him to never being forgiven. He was guilty for no other reason than he was told that he should be, he must be, and his sickness proved it.

He lay at the feet of God, helpless, waiting for eternal wrath. He received eternal life, and the God of his expectations died as surely as the God of Jesus was resurrected in this cruel god's place.

He could never rise from his bed until his heart was healed. Why? Because all hope had been stolen from him. Now he could do more than walk. He could dance with the joy of the unmerited and unearned love of God. He looked into the eyes of God expecting death and saw life.

He looked into the eyes of God expecting death—and saw life.

This is the miracle that took place in Simon Peter's house. A man returned to his home knowing who God truly was. He had unlearnt who he thought God to be.

Jesus had come to the story of his pain. It was his heart that was paralysed. The Pharisees went away, the crowd murmured among themselves, the disciples wished for a better 'spin'. But one man's heart danced!

There were more 'cripples' that Jesus was looking for, more who must hear the message. These ones were not part of the crowd. They didn't belong in the multitudes that milled around Simon's house in Capernaum. Jesus' message was for them as well.

Now the confusion that began in Simon's house grew into contradictions. Jesus opened his arms to those who had been excluded. Following him was now more than miracles—it was a challenge to reactions that were once quite normal, understandable and defensible. Jesus accepted those whom the crowd rejected.

After these things He went out and saw a tax collector named Levi, sitting at the tax office. And He said to him, 'Follow Me.'

A tax collector! Even today tax collectors are not particularly popular men. How many tax collectors were at your last New Year's Eve party? In Jesus' time they were held in great contempt. They were the enemies of the poor, the lowest of the low. When the kingdom came, everyone in Capernaum would have expected the tax collectors to be excluded. In fact, I can imagine that everyone in Capernaum would have hoped for much worse to befall them at the hands of the Messiah. Everyone would have 'expected' this.

But not this Messiah. Not Jesus.

Levi, whom Jesus renames Matthew (meaning 'gift of God'—such beautiful irony), held a party for Jesus. The 'poor in spirit' had just been offered the kingdom, personally. Levi was astounded. He had already heard the words as they echoed from every hopeless heart in Capernaum. They fell like rain on his dry soul. But it was too good to be true, and he had dismissed it by believing he was poorer than the poor in spirit. To be honest, those who had heard the words from Jesus' mouth would have agreed with him. They were poor, but when they looked at Levi's ilk, they comforted themselves that they were not *that* poor.

It is tragic when true hope is snatched out of the hearts of the hopeless. It is more tragic when it is by the hands of those who are equally hopeless. What heals one man, is then denied to his brother. Sometimes I think we are like terminally ill patients all connected to the same life support machines but spending our time arguing about the colour of our pyjamas and the names of our diseases.

Levi was sitting in his accursed office. He was longing for salvation to come to his house and the house of his friends. In the notes in the Bible I have pulled down from my shelf is the following comment concerning Levi and his friends:

> Tax collectors and sinners are often grouped together, and signify those people who by vocation or morality place them-

selves outside the society of God's covenant people. By consorting with such persons labelled as sinners, Jesus had crossed the Jewish boundary lines. Tax collectors and sinners were not even to be taught the statutes of God since their vocation and lifestyle made them ritually unclean.

Vocation, lifestyle and morality. How many Levis do you know?

The Jews had judged these tax collectors and their sinner friends as unworthy. Unworthy to share the society of God's covenant people. Unworthy to partake of the blessings, the promises, the hopes and the dreams. They were outcasts. They were refused teaching and fellowship.

They were damned. God was barred to them.

Why? Because the things that they did rendered them 'unacceptable'. Who decided this? Those who were considered the 'doorkeepers' to all that was good and godly—the ones who enforced the law.

But these enforcers were not alone. Levi and his friends had heard the words of Jesus only third or fourth hand, because no God-fearing Jew of any kind would have anything to do with them. Who were the God-fearing Jews in Capernaum? Surely those who were looking for the Messiah. If the whole of Capernaum society was built on interpretations and expectations concerning God and who he accepted and rejected, then surely those gathered at the feet of Jesus were just as willing 'doorkeepers' as those who actually enforced the law.

In following Jesus, 'forsaking all' takes on a new meaning.

What was glorious to Levi was inglorious to Capernaum. They expected a Messiah who would affirm their beliefs. Jesus walked in the other direction. What did they do? They sought miracles, but a tax collector? That was too much. And what were the disciples saying? Suddenly they had a new 'brother'. What were his credentials to join this godly band of missionaries? If Jesus called Levi, what did that say of them?

It's not so cut and dry, is it? In following Jesus, 'forsaking all' takes on a new meaning.

Jesus and his growing band of personally chosen disciples went to Levi's party. It was the first time they had ever darkened his doorstep, and they must have been extremely uncomfortable.

Were they tempted to ask Jesus to put a 'spin' on his ministry? 'Let's concentrate on the miracles. The people like miracles. Miracles draw a crowd. Let's not offend the scribes and Pharisees. They are influential men. Let's stay away from controversial social groups. Better to avoid the issue than get caught up in it.' Surely there must have been conversations like this as those who followed Jesus tried to swallow Levi's food and wine.

> And when the scribes and Pharisees saw Him eating with the tax collectors and sinners, they said to His disciples, 'How is it that He eats and drinks with tax collectors and sinners?'

In other words, what are you doing following this 'sinner'? Peter, Andrew, James and John, for goodness' sake come to your senses and go home to your families, go back to your boats, leave this issue with us and we will deal with it.

But Jesus heard them and replied:

> 'Those who are well have no need of a physician, but those who are sick. I did not come to call the righteous, but sinners, to repentance.'

There was no 'spin' on this statement. The fishermen swallowed hard. Jesus had just awarded them Levi's righteousness, or lack of it! These were hard words for those who were 'pursuing righteousness' according to the law.

Levi and his friends, however, had been restored to society. They had been given hope. The outcast was brought in, the reject accepted. And every Levi from that day on would hear this same message . . . as long as the new doorkeepers didn't forget their own sinfulness.

For the doorkeepers too had been expecting a Messiah who had been presented to them in terms of judgment. They too had no hope, so all they could do was comfort each other. A Messiah in town was just another reason for the spiritually zealous to become more so. Every revival brings with it a revival of self-righteousness as each worshipper seeks to earn their way into the kingdom of their own spiritual desires. Works of 'worship' are performed as once again a community seeks to redeem itself by passing self-righteous judgment on others.

'God is coming, so we'd better clean up the town.'

Levi and his friends were the first to feel the sting of the brooms. I can imagine their cynicism at first as they heard the news that Jesus was performing miracles in Capernaum. They had already made up their minds. Or rather, their minds were made up for them when God was snatched away from their hope-starved hearts by those who were sure of their own blessedness. (One would think that the cross would have ended this tragedy. But now the same thing is so often done 'in the name of Jesus'. How tragic it is that we are still blind to the hammer and nails in our hands, our own naked self-righteousness.)

Jesus, however, made a beeline for Levi and his friends. They saw who God really was, and those who thought they knew went away in judgmental, self-righteous disappointment.

Imagine the hearts of this merry crowd of social pariahs. God had come to sit at the table of the outcast! He was drinking their wine and eating their food! Because God *was* an excluded outcast!

The journey continued. Jesus was now followed by many groups of people. There were those closest to him who had been 'called', struggling with the credentials of their calling and with the identity of their fellow disciples. There were those craving a miracle—the lame, the sick, the oppressed and the dying. There were those enjoying the 'show', fighting for the best seats closest to the front so they could see the action. And there were those who were captivated by this man's life, those for whom everything he said was simple evidence of what their hearts were hearing for the first time. Their eyes had been confronted with the truth, and deep inside their broken, failed souls they were finally seeing hope dawn where they never believed, let alone expected, it could be.

And then there were those who were incensed at all that was going on. Their rules, regulations, laws and precepts were in tatters as Jesus shredded their moral and social codes. They 'knew the truth'. They had 'researched' this Jesus, Joseph's son, from Nazareth. They were already planning to destroy him, for their minds were made up. They were simply waiting for the inevitable. Jesus would say something one day that would turn the crowd against him, and then they would pounce. Until then they would question everything he said. They were longing for the 'true' God to come, and they knew that every threat to his identity must be dealt with, ruthlessly. Capernaum must know the truth about this Jesus. It was their business to point it out.

They wouldn't fail.

8

Outcasts

Do you remember the story about a little girl on the North Coast of New South Wales who had tragically contracted AIDS? She was an 'innocent', a child whose future had been stolen by a cruel twist of 'fate'. Yes, I know that Christians don't like that word, but how would you prefer her parents to interpret their daughter's illness? This little girl attended the local pre-school, a happy child with long blond hair, a toothy smile, lots of friends and a time bomb ticking away inside her. Words cannot describe the pain, the fear, the immense loss her mum and dad must have felt.

When this unfortunate pre-schooler was diagnosed, the parents of her little friends were informed of the terrible tragedy. Of course, the community opened its homes to this devastated family. These parents arranged for this poor sick child to be showered with love and affection. They supported this grief-stricken couple, determining to make what was left of her brief life as joyous as possible, filling every moment with the best memories. Of course.

Not!

The little girl and her family were kicked out of town. They were humiliated by the intensity of the campaign run by the parents of her little friends to flush this contaminated scourge from the antiseptic corridors of their children's pre-school. She died in New Zealand.

On the news this morning were two interesting items. One

concerned a well-known businessman who has just been released from gaol. The other concerned a geriatric old man from Eastern Europe who over half a century ago was possibly a very guilty party in a heinous chapter of history. This old man is being hunted down, and the editorials and radio talk-back will be full of venom.

Both men are horribly guilty, no doubt about it. Indefensible acts. Both men, however, are someone's sons, and some son's father. Both men live in a world where they must take the venom from a society that covers its own sins.

We find it so easy to judge others but far harder to judge ourselves. Every 'afternoon edition' is full of the wrath and indignation of faceless editors, programmers and spokespersons who believe they have the responsibility to shape public opinion. Public opinion in turn shapes a culture, a culture that raises children to become adults who run pre-schools. These editorials will continue to spruik their lynch mob morality while a little girl's persecutors raise children who tragically may grow into their parents' image. Society will turn its back while other respectable businessmen bankrupt families with economic rationalism, and our nation will continue to judge Eastern Europeans while steadfastly refusing to acknowledge the genocide that occurred in our own land.

What do you do with a Messiah who performs miracles yet refuses to take 'your side'?

What is the problem here?

We want to be on the right side. We want our enemies to be on the wrong side, judged and sentenced, ridiculed and removed. If anyone should ever challenge us, we question their morality and judge them as well. After all, God is on our side.

He'd better be, otherwise we will judge him too!

Listen to the talk back radio and hear the pain of our nation.

Jesus came to Capernaum and all Capernaum came to Jesus.

But before very long, it was clear that this Messiah was not on their side.

What do you do with a Messiah who performs the most wonderful of miracles, opening blind eyes and healing paralytics, yet steadfastly refuses to take 'your side'? What would you do with a Messiah who opened Stevie Wonder's eyes in the morning, raised Princess Di to life at lunch, told Christopher Reeve to walk home before dinner, then went to an AIDS hospice to embrace, befriend and heal desperate and dying young men—before returning to commend the faith of General Wiranto of the Indonesian army and dine at his table?

Would you wake up the next morning, tune into the morning talk back, listen to scores of disappointed disciples and disillusioned devotees, and then give a large donation to his ministry?

Think carefully. Who are *you* expecting God to be?

Jesus was turning Capernaum upside down. By now he had performed some miracles, called a tax collector, shared a meal with his new disciple's mates, and preached on a hillside.

Behind the scenes, however, the murmuring was gaining in intensity.

People close to Jesus and closer to the four fishermen were talking behind their hands. The ministry needed a 'press secretary', they whispered again, a 'spin doctor'. Some may have been worried that the momentum of the last few days would cause a loss of wisdom, reason and popularity. Jesus needed influence. He must make friends with the influential, otherwise his mission was doomed before it got off the ground. Were there suggestions of 'let's stop, take stock, then plan a strategy that is less confrontational'?

What would be your advice as, on the one side, the most amazing things are taking place and, on the other, just about every influential leader in town is being insulted and the 'cause' is becoming increasingly isolated? How would you deal with the erosion of Jesus' credibility? If you were the assistant minister in a new church, how would you deal with your reputation in a town that was accusing your superior of 'demon possession'? And these accusations were not coming from the 'normal sectors' of expected opposition but from the local ministers' fraternal? If you were the deputy leader of a missionary team that had been sent to Capernaum and these reports were relayed back to 'International Missionary Headquarters', what would the next fax tell you to do?

Jesus was unmoved. He was either not listening or not aware or simply didn't care. He had work to accomplish, and its results had nothing to do with establishing a sense of momentum, popularity and influence. His work continually confounded the expectations of his disciples and the multitudes. Jesus showed this expectant world that their expectations were not going to be met. Jesus refused to bow to the pressure of advisers. He would not be subject to the polls. He did not appoint a 'press secretary' or a 'spin doctor'. He was not driven by populist theories.

God was not in the middle of a 'process of development'. Jesus' work was the revealing of the absolute nature and character of God—the One who is and was and is to come. And that message was final. It hadn't changed since the beginning of time and it couldn't change. Therefore it was the expectations of Capernaum that must surrender. From the scribes and Pharisees down to the lame and the lepers, all expectations must bow to the reality of God in Jesus.

> When He had come down from the mountain, great multitudes followed Him. And behold, a leper came and worshipped Him, saying, 'Lord, if You are willing, You can make me clean.' Then Jesus put out His hand and touched him, saying, 'I am willing; be cleansed.' Immediately his leprosy was cleansed.

In the past, whenever I read this passage I thought about the miracle. But now I want to think about the leper. To do this, can I ask you to do one thing? It is what I have just done. I stopped my two-fingered typing, let the screensaver wash away my words, and opened Leviticus 13 and 14. Please put this book down and read the 'life of a leper' described in these two chapters.

No picnic, is it?

A leper came to Jesus. He had already gone through all the requirements of the law. Words fail me as I think of the heartbreak that this poor man and his family had endured from the minute he found the first sore. The appointments with the priest, the waiting periods, seven days, another seven days, another seven days. The fear and finality of the diagnosis and judgment. The unembraced 'good-byes' as he turned from his house, his wife and his children and walked away, never to return. Life would never be the same again. All that was ahead for this poor wretch was the certainty of a lonely death. His life was destroyed. He was sentenced to hopeless humiliation, isolation and deprivation. This man would have ached for human contact. His lonely nights would have been filled with dreams of affection, just as a thirsty man dreams of water. His family, his wife and children, his parents and friends all had to turn away. He was an outcast.

His life was now solely determined by the placard that hung around his neck like a noose. His past was obscured by his disease. He was now simply 'Leper'.

Imagine this is you. What kind of life must you live? Your family has burnt your clothes. Your village has cast you out. Your God has forsaken you. Your body refuses to die. You have become the only witness to a horrid physical deterioration that will disfigure and maim you. You are repulsive. Your own reflection horrifies you. You know you will die alone, outcast and rejected, and your remains will be burnt and the ashes buried. Your enduring memorial will carry one word: 'Leper'.

What questions would you ask of God? What prayers would you pray? How could you not despair?

In 1993 a friend of mine contracted AIDS. I visited him in hospital. He was in a ward containing six beds. Six young men, ashen-faced, hollow-cheeked and dying. My heart cried that day. I felt helpless as the hope that I had in my heart was irrelevant to these men. Why? Because God had been made their enemy, and I was one of his supporters.

AIDS is a tragedy, an untimely death that stalks the strong and the virile, a disease that hides itself in the embraces of relationship. In some sections of our society, these dying men are judged and rejected. Their disease is seen as the judgment of God. Standards of morality are pushed into their hollow faces as their prayers are snatched from their broken hearts. As they lie dying on their beds, they are sentenced and dismissed by this depraved, cancerous mentality of callous, self-righteous indifference. They are shown a 'faith' that takes on the same morality as the pre-schoolers' parents, who refused to see, let alone dry, the tears of a little girl who didn't even understand her disease.

When their funerals are over and their grief-stricken friends and lovers go home, what kind of God are they expecting? What would they think of him after everything that has been said and done in his name? How can we call our ministry 'Light' when it is so dark? It is no 'Festival' to these men and their bereaved families.

The leper said to Jesus, 'If you are willing, you can make me clean.'

Jesus said, 'I am willing . . .'

But Jesus was more than willing to cleanse and heal. He was willing to touch and share.

It is easy for us to pray for healing, sitting in comfortable chairs in middle-class homes. But it is Christlike to embrace the disease and the diseased, touching the untouchables in their palliative care wards. There is an enormous difference. One dispenses grace prayerfully, the other gives grace personally. One gathers to pray, the other goes to love. One asks God to answer, the other sees themselves as God's answer.

Please, don't ever stop praying. But I beg of you, never let prayer be enough to silence your compassion, giving you permission to withdraw your arms that can embrace and your hands that can touch.

Jesus said he was willing to cleanse, but it was what he *did* that was really important. He touched the leper. Jesus was willing to cross the boundaries clearly set out in Leviticus 14 and enforced rigidly ever since. He was willing to step over the requirements of the law and touch this man. Every eye was on him. And as the crowd watched, they were suddenly very concerned about the 'what ifs'.

'What if the leper isn't cleansed?' 'What if Jesus becomes leprous?' 'What if the hands that healed me yesterday are contaminated today?' Then the multitude would scatter as fast as it gathered, and Jesus would be hounded out of town.

Jesus would become 'unclean'.

Imagine the self-righteous pleasure of the scribes and Pharisees as they demanded that 'Jesus the leper' cry out, 'Unclean! Unclean!' They would have led him through the streets, bound and chained by the sentence of the law. Streets that once rejoiced but now shrank from the carpenter from Nazareth as he became despised and rejected.

Jesus risked everything. He placed it all on the line: his friends, his disciples, his ministry and his future. All for one man. His love for this leper gave him no choice. The choice had been made in eternity, and every act echoed its final fulfilment.

Jesus touched the leper.

The crowd shrank back in horror.

God came out of the comfort and safety of eternity and clothed himself with a body so that his heart could have hands to touch the broken, affection-starved bodies of the lepers, embracing their rejection, holding their pain and shielding them from judgment. God came to join the lepers.

Jesus shows us a love that goes beyond risk. A love so selfless that it will deny itself for the sake of just one other. A love that will turn away from an adoring multitude to reach one solitary, hopeless heart. Jesus shows us that the worth of one individual soul is greater than a multitude's approval. True revival comes to one heart. It is this love that shows the reality of God among us. The human heart is humiliated by this love, for it forever shows us our own shallowness. The great depths of human compassion, the most wonderful stories of selfless sacrifice, are still overshadowed by the love of God that comes from eternity for one leper, forever making 'one' the object of 'all'.

Jesus shows us a love so selfless that it will deny itself for the sake of just one other.

Jesus was this love that came to meet the needs and bathe the wounds of one broken individual. He was God's body. Where is that body now? Can the 'lepers' still see him apart from the multitude? Or have the needs of the crowd hidden him from view?

The leper saw Jesus extend his hand towards him. His mind raced. 'Surely not! Jesus couldn't touch me. He would be unclean. He wouldn't dare.' The leper saw it clearly. But Jesus' hand reached out, and the leper knew: Jesus was willing not only to *cleanse* a leper but to *become* a leper! His mind exploded with an astonishing thought: was Jesus about to join him outside the city walls in the leper colony, hiding in the caves with the other lepers? (In the hills surrounding the western shore of the Sea of Galilee, you can still see the caves where these wretched people lived and died.) The leper's mind raced with the imagery of Jesus returning with him, clothed in leprous rags, holding what was left of his hand and embracing his leprous friends.

If this man was God, then God had come to be a leper so that lepers would never die alone. Oh, the indescribable joy of it! Let this echo through every leper colony, into every AIDS ward, until the news is heard in every town. God has come to embrace the unembraceable! He has come to join them!

He has even come to join us as we live in the 'leprosy' of our judgmental attitudes. He is willing to touch us, too. Can we see that we also are 'unclean'?

Jesus touched the leper, and immediately the leprosy was gone and he was clean. Now, having read through Leviticus 14, 'Rituals for Cleansing Healed Lepers', you will realise that this poor man still had a long way to go. But we know that eventually the day would dawn when he would walk into his house to embrace and be embraced, to play with his children and to sleep in his own bed in the arms of his wife. And this glorious hope was overshadowed by an even greater truth. Before he went to the priest to make the offerings prescribed by the law, the beauty of everything that had just happened dawned on him afresh. Jesus had given him more than life. He had shown him the enormity of God's love. He now knew that he had been accepted by God, totally and unconditionally, even while still leprous. The healing came after the acceptance. He went home to his family carrying in his heart an awareness of God that had overturned everything he ever knew or expected of God.

The 'Leper's Messiah' had come. When Jesus touched the leper, he demanded of us that every leprous expectation concerning him be healed. It is our hearts that are sick. Our concepts and judgments prove the leprosy of our souls. When we look at Jesus through our leprous flesh, we can then rejoice with the leper. When we see this grace, we can then clearly see ourselves. When we see ourselves, we can see the decay of our flesh in all that we have said and done to our fellow sufferers. We can never judge again, because if we do we are simply refusing to look at our own reflection.

I guess the crowd was simply grateful that the man was healed so they could continue to seek their miracles and touch Jesus. The disciples and their friends breathed a sigh of relief: 'Phew, that was close!'

Worse was yet to come.

Jesus enters Dili. He is wearing the uniform of an Australian military chaplain. He comes to a crowded marketplace and an Indonesian officer comes to him, pleading . . .

Jesus enters Kosovo. He is wearing the uniform of a United Nations peace keeper, and a Yugoslavian officer comes to him, pleading . . .

Jesus enters liberated Paris. He is wearing the uniform of an Allied soldier, and a Nazi commander comes to him, pleading . . .

> Now when Jesus had entered Capernaum, a centurion came to Him, pleading with Him, saying, 'Lord, my servant is lying at home paralysed, dreadfully tormented.'
>
> And Jesus said to him, 'I will come and heal him.'

The crowd was stunned. Someone down the back yelled, 'Whose side are you on?' The faces of the fishermen were white with fear. The scribes and Pharisees had their moment. He had gone too far.

The centurion looked around. He was a political man. He knew the trap that somehow this strangely naive miracle worker had fallen into. He looked at Jesus, dismayed: 'Whatever you do, don't come *with* me. Couldn't you have put some conditions on this? Do you know what you've just done?' The centurion had just heard the most courageous words from the bravest man he had ever seen. 'How could you even think, let alone say, that *you* will come with *me*?'

It was quite likely that the nationalistic zealots of Capernaum, and every other occupied Jewish town, made many collaborators regret ever having anything to do with centurions and their accursed army. Perhaps the centurion's servant had suffered at the hands of these men. Surely, being the 'employee' of Rome would have excluded his servant from everyone and everything in Capernaum. Like the tax collector Levi and his friends, this servant's vocation rendered him an outcast. Did the compassionate heart of this Roman grieve for his servant's broken life? The servant had lost family and friends. He was barred from the synagogue. He was excluded from his nation, banished from his tribe and rejected by his God. He was now in agony—and the centurion had to do something.

A strange reversal of roles had happened in the centurion's household. The 'served' had become the 'servant'. Perhaps he was hoping for Jesus to pray or, at best, use his influence to restore his servant back to society so he could die in the arms of his loved ones. He was not prepared for Jesus' answer. In the middle of a crowd full of hatred for Rome and nationalistic expectations for Jesus, the hearts of these two leaders met.

Both were servants. Both would serve to the death. Both were risking all for the one they loved. Both were prepared to pay any price.

The centurion was not expecting this from Jesus. He was prepared for the consequences of his own love, but he wasn't coming to ask Jesus to share them. He would never presume this of any man. He was a soldier. He knew responsibility. So he now sought an appropriate 'political' solution, trying to spare Jesus the 'guilt by association'. 'Jesus, you don't need to come personally. I know my place, and so does my poor servant. We have no choice, but you do. Protect yourself, your followers and your cause and just say the word, I know that will be enough. It has to be, it is the best that I could possibly expect.'

The centurion tries to shield Jesus from judgment.

How Christlike.

The centurion answered and said, 'Lord, I am not worthy that You should come under my roof. But only speak a word, and my servant will be healed. For I also am a man under authority, having soldiers under me. And I say to this one, "Go," and he goes; and to another, "Come," and he comes; and to my servant, "Do this," and he does it.'

I am startled by his opening remarks. We usually interpret this story as a message about the centurion's understanding of spiritual authority. We cheer because this Roman recognised Jesus' power over sickness and disease. We think that this affirmation of our expectations of God's power is all about the miraculous. We eagerly await the day when we will do the same (in his name, of course!).

But again, we have missed the point. Yes, the story is about authority, but it is not what we expect. Jesus shows us what true authority is as he chooses to lay down his life for others. True authority is exercised in serving. True authority says, 'Take my life, not his.' This story is about servanthood—the 'served' becoming the 'servants' and the 'servants' becoming the 'served'.

No wonder Jesus wanted to go with this Roman. He had found a 'soul mate'. We have turned this glorious meeting of hearts into a theology of power, missing the 'word becoming flesh' in the actions of these two men.

The centurion said to Jesus, while the whole crowd looked on: 'I am not worthy.' What an amazing statement to come from a Roman officer powerful enough to have a servant and soldiers under him. This amounted to an act of 'surrender'. He came and bowed his authority, position, power and influence before Jesus. He came 'serving and to serve'. He did this in the sight of a multitude in occupied Capernaum.

This was incredibly brave.

He could have been arrested. His statement was treasonous.

He, a servant of Rome, had laid his power and position at the feet of two men, first his servant, now Jesus.

'Greater love has no one than this, than to lay down one's life for his friends.'

The centurion was putting his life on the line for his sick servant. He didn't gain anything from this; in fact, he could very well have lost everything. He didn't want to 'sit on the right or the left' of Jesus when he came into his kingdom. He didn't seek to preserve his authority by negotiating a coup for his own political gain. He simply loved his servant and wanted him to be well. He was simply moved with compassion.

What wonderful faith!

When Jesus heard this, we're told, he marvelled. And wouldn't you? It was so unexpected. And Jesus said to his followers:

> 'Assuredly, I say to you, I have not found such great faith, even in all Israel! And I say to you that many will come from east and west, and sit down with Abraham, Isaac and Jacob in the kingdom of heaven. But the sons of the kingdom will be cast out into outer darkness. There will be weeping and gnashing of teeth.'
>
> Then he said to the centurion, 'Go your way; and as you have believed, so let it be done for you.' And his servant was healed at that very hour.

Jesus gave the centurion more than he came for. Look again. The centurion came in selfless, sacrificial love, laying down everything, only seeking for his servant to be healed. Jesus promised the same selfless, sacrificial love to the centurion. In saying this, Jesus was offering himself back to this centurion just as the centurion offered himself to Jesus. Deeper than words, the hearts of these two men met and the 'cross of the sacrificial servant' was proclaimed before a crowd that was

You cannot execute a man who has chosen to sacrifice himself.

totally unaware of the depth of this eternal transaction.

All authority is disarmed by this love. You cannot execute a man who has chosen to sacrifice himself. You can only fulfil his choice. He has the ultimate authority and he uses it to be the ultimate servant.

What of the other player in this encounter—the servant? He was lying in bed, tormented and paralysed. He had been told of the actions of his master. Suddenly his limbs were free, his torment gone. Before long he heard the story from his master's lips. What thoughts raced through the mind of this man who had been rejected by 'the sons of the kingdom' because of his treacherous vocation? The servant learnt the love of Christ through a Roman centurion, an enemy of Israel, by discovering his true worth as one who was 'died for'.

Meanwhile, the crowd was ignorant. God had come to them living a love that knew no borders, no prejudice, no social stigmas and no limits. This love could have overthrown their fear of Rome just as it overthrew Rome in the heart of the centurion. This love could have freed them from their enslavement to 'knowing right' and 'being right'. If they could have recognised the poverty of their judgments and expectations, they could have rejoiced in the unconditionality of the kingdom of God—a kingdom that welcomes all to serve one another, all to be served. A kingdom that is enthroned by an outpouring of love.

It is this unexpected love that brings Jesus to our place as we marvel at his love for us. This love defuses our hatred and prejudice because our enemies are loved equally with us. And as this Roman shows us, our enemies can also love equally.

But the multitudes, unfortunately, preferred to judge the one who disappointed them. As they saw it, in refusing to take sides Jesus had actually taken the side of the Roman. They were incensed at what he had said. He had made a centurion into a son of the kingdom while excommunicating those they believed were the real sons of Abraham, Isaac and Jacob. Once again, it was too much.

If only they could have seen the truth that lay beneath this wonderful meeting. The core of the issue is the simple question: who are the 'sons of the kingdom'? The centurion answered them with his acts of love.

The scribes and Pharisees could not believe their good fortune. Jesus had ruined his ministry before it had even started. Sooner or later, they assured themselves, even his disciples would have sufficient doubts to betray him. When that happened, the whole nation would have nothing to do with him. Not even the Rome of this centurion would come to his aid.

That time would come.

9

John the Baptist

> *The voice of one crying in the wilderness:*
> *'Prepare the way of the Lord . . .'*

John the Baptist was in the wilderness baptising. All his life, his heart had echoed with the words of the prophets. His conception was announced to his father Zacharias—through the lips of the angel Gabriel, no less—in the words of the prophet Malachi:

> 'He will also go before Him in the spirit and power of Elijah, "to turn the hearts of the fathers to the children," and the disobedient to the wisdom of the just, to make ready a people prepared for the Lord.'

His father prophesied at his birth:

> 'And you, child, will be called the prophet of the Highest; for you will go before the face of the Lord to prepare his ways'.

When the Jews sent priests and Levites from Jerusalem to ask John, 'Who are you?', he answered by quoting the prophecy of Isaiah 40:

> I am 'The voice of one crying in the wilderness: "Make straight the way of the Lord."'

You could easily say that John the Baptist's life was framed by prophecy. From an early age he would have heard his mother's story of her first meeting with her cousin, the pregnant Mary. He would have known that he was filled with the Spirit while still in his mother's womb. His concepts of the Messiah from this story alone would have been momentous. His childhood and teenage years would have been filled with these words and stories and prophecies.

The young John must have had great dreams and greater expectations. He went into the wilderness preaching repentance. He lived a strict life with a strong message. He must have appeared like an Old Testament prophet as he stood by the banks of the Jordan River, waiting for the One who was the fulfilment of all the prophecies. All his life he was waiting for the day when the Messiah would step onto the stage of history.

Can you imagine the conversations as John and his disciples gathered around the fire waiting for the Messiah? Can you imagine their excitement and anticipation? What was he going to look like? What wonderful things was he going to do? What was his kingdom going to be like? Would they have a role in it?

Questions, anticipations, expectations.

One magnificent day, Jesus came to the Jordan to be baptised by John. He simply arrived, unannounced, stepping into John's expectant hopes and dreams. All that John had spoken of and dreamt about was now reality. Standing in front of him was the Messiah—his Messiah!

John and his disciples were beyond themselves with excitement. Suddenly all the prophecies, stories, prayers and longings were coming together in a man called Jesus of Nazareth. John looked on in awe as the Spirit of God descended in the form of a dove on the head of Jesus and he heard the voice of God thundering from the heavens. What was he thinking as this man stood before him, dripping wet, just like every other man he had baptised during those long years—yet so very different?

Immediately Jesus was led by the Spirit into the wilderness, but John stayed at the Jordan baptising. Now, though, everything had changed. How on earth did John contain himself? For a brief instant the Messiah was before him. <u>For a few short minutes John looked into the face of God.</u> He saw, he heard . . . and then Jesus was gone! The crowds still came, but for John life was different. No longer was he looking forward. Now he could look back and remember the sights and sounds as his world was firmly imprinted with the reality of God in Jesus.

Night and day he strained to remember the sound of Jesus' voice. He heard the words in his sleep. He recounted them to anyone who would listen, daily, hourly. Every minute John scanned the crowd, searching through the sea of expectant faces, looking again for Jesus. Every morning dawned with the hope that before the day ended he would see his Messiah again.

John was beside himself with a greater longing than he had ever known.

Forty days and forty nights went by. His whole life up until this point had been waiting, but now everything that went before—hopes, dreams, prophecies and expectations—all faded into insignificance. *He* had come. The prophecies had been fulfilled, and John had seen their fulfilment. With his own eyes he had seen the One whom the nation had groaned for, ached for, prayed for. He had embraced him in the Jordan.

John was beside himself with a greater longing than he had ever known. His disciples gathered around him as he told the story again and again.

Some time during this 'pregnant month', the two brothers, Andrew and Simon, who were already John's disciples, arrived from Capernaum. They were immediately caught up in the stories running like fire through every conversation at the Jordan. The news had reached their home town as it was carried in the hearts of those returning from pilgrimage. So the brothers had taken leave of their partners, their boats and their families and had come down the Jordan, looking for the Messiah.

They had much time to talk as they walked the long road south. Their conversation was filled with all manner of hopes and dreams. The Messiah had come, out of the hills of Galilee! Of all places that God could have come, he had come to their land, their home and their people. They could scarcely believe they had been born in the right place at the right time.

After forty days and forty nights, with John counting each one faithfully since Jesus' baptism, the Messiah returned. John could not contain his excitement as he yelled exultantly for all the world to hear: 'Behold! The Lamb of God who takes away the sins of the world!'

Andrew was standing with John and his heart skipped a beat. He looked up and saw Jesus.

How many times throughout Andrew's remaining years did he speak of this moment, the moment when he first saw the Messiah? Years would pass and that moment would not dim. I can imagine Andrew in his last days, with all the memories of three years with Jesus and all the years that followed, still remembering this first day.

He impulsively started to follow Jesus. What else could he do? The moment must not slip from his grasp.

And then it happened: Jesus spoke to him. 'What do you seek?'

Andrews blurted out a silly reply. 'Where are you staying?'

Jesus answered him and said the fateful words that were forever sealed in his heart: 'Come and see.'

Andrew saw and heard. Then he raced off to find his brother Simon. Together, for the first time, they gathered at the feet of Jesus. No wonder they were ruined for fishing!

Jesus moved on, back to Cana, back to a wedding. Andrew

and Simon eventually found their way back to Capernaum, to wait again for Jesus. And John continued to baptise. He had been preparing the way. He had no other instructions, so he continued to prepare the way. Now, however, he knew who he was preparing the way for. His mind raced with images of salvation, deliverance, redemption and peace.

As time went on he heard about the miracles, the multitudes and the growing number of converts and disciples. Many of his own disciples travelled north to Galilee to hear Jesus and returned with the most wonderful tales. John glorified God.

However, not all the news was as he expected, and not everything went the way he wished.

One day John was arrested and put in prison. While awaiting sentence, he sent a message to Jesus by two of his disciples:

'Are You the Coming One, or do we look for another?'

What had happened to John to make him wonder such a thing? What had clouded everything he once believed concerning Jesus? What made him doubt so severely that he called two of his disciples and shared with them his concerns, sending them to Jesus to find the answers?

John had longed for the Christ, but when he heard *everything* that Jesus was saying and doing, his heart filled with doubts. He heard the 'other stories' and started to ask himself some questions:

'Would the Messiah *really* say and do such things?'
'Would the Messiah *really* have these kind of friends?'
'Would I have so many doubts if he were *really* the Messiah?'

Broken, disillusioned and imprisoned, John eventually had to face the awful doubt that had grown in his heart. Was Jesus the *real* Messiah?

Jesus was not the Messiah John had expected, and John was now surrounded by broken dreams. What a horrible thought.

John was alone in prison, his ministry over, his opportunities all gone, and the one reason why he had endured so much now appeared to be horribly wrong. He had placed everything on the line for Jesus. He never even thought to question him. He believed from the instant he saw him at the Jordan.

Time and time again John went over the events. God had told him: 'Upon whom you see the Spirit descending, and remaining on Him, this is He who baptises with the Holy Spirit.' He asked himself again: 'Did I see the Spirit descend and remain on the head of Jesus? Did I hear the voice of God?' For an instant the memory was fresh and clear . . . then he looked at all he had seen and heard since, and the doubts and fears descended like a black cloud.

'Have I given my life for a false Messiah? Have I made the greatest mistake of all time?'

So many of us reach the lowest point of life, the point at which everything that can go wrong, has gone wrong. All we have is our faith to give us hope and comfort. Our faith in God is a rock that supports all we are and all we do. Even though 'the heavens may tremble and fall', we can still say, with faith, that we love God. When all is lost, we still confess that we are able to be found. In 1993, I wrote a song called 'Have Faith in God'. It was written for my father who had just been diagnosed with cancer. It was also written for me, his son, as I started to trust God with my dad's life. This song has brought me so much comfort, and it brought my father and my family great peace as he was slowly taken from us. I have so many letters that express similar emotions. God held our hands, dried our tears and gave us hope for a new day.

There is a place, however, where all this hope and comfort disappears. This place is the prison where we suddenly fear that even our faith has been in vain. Where do we go when our faith seems futile? What do we do when we come to the point of questioning God's reality and identity? Who is left to comfort us?

We are truly alone.

This is where John the Baptist found himself.

It was a terrible, lonely, hopeless place of indescribable despair.

Have we made a tragic mistake trying to present the normal, frail, doubting human beings we meet in the Gospels as fearless saints? Have we robbed the gospel of its greatest colour by reducing Jesus to fit into our monochromatic expectations, ignoring the doubts of Baptisers and disciples? Have we attributed to these men faith and insight that they never deserved, and in so doing sentenced ourselves to guiltily hide our own doubt, hastily prescribing a renewed discipline of study until the 'heresies' of our fear and disillusionment disappear? How repressed is our faith if we cannot take comfort from the doubts of those who saw him face to face?

The life of God is frail if it needs to be protected from our journeys through doubt and fear.

The life of God is frail if it needs to be protected from humanity's journeys through dark doubts and fears. Although Jesus sought out his disciples, and although he was found with the tax collectors and sinners, are we afraid that all of a sudden he may recoil from our doubts and hide himself from us?

It is so clear to me that it wasn't so clear to those who saw it all, and this gives me such wonderful encouragement. Why? Because it is when *we* are confronted with *our* broken expectations that *we* finally have to choose.

'Will the real Jesus please stand up?'

Everyone who is confronted with the reality of who God really is in Jesus, then has to confront their mistaken beliefs in who they thought he would and should be.

John now had a wonderful awakening. God was not in the image of his expectations. God was in the image of his Son, Jesus. John had to throw away his dreams and look at Jesus without prejudice, without preconditions, and see for himself who God really is and what God really does. John's expectations didn't challenge Jesus; they challenged John. John had to change his 'image' of God.

That is the choice. Our image or his?

The things that caused John to stumble were the same things that would cause us to doubt—and surely that is why John and his questions have been so faithfully recorded for us. First there was the calling of that tax collector. John hadn't seen Levi at the Jordan seeking forgiveness and a good washing.

John was frankly shocked. Levi invited Jesus to *his* house, and Jesus had gone! Surely Jesus should have invited Levi to accompany him to somewhere more acceptable. It is one thing having suspect friends; it is an entirely different thing to sit at *their* table in *their* house. Jesus should have made time for Levi in his diary, perhaps once a week for counselling, and when progress had been made, introduced Levi to a few pastors who would have him over to their place for dinner. When Levi had sufficiently 'brought forth the fruit' to accompany his change of heart (and you must be sure these days), perhaps he could serve as a 'doorkeeper' on Sundays. He would be warned not to lay hands on anyone, of course, but at least he would be a good testimony to the skills of the pastoral department! He could even invite his former friends to church, but it would be advisable for him to break off all social contact with them until his faith gained maturity. Usually this is after he has passed the 'New Christians Class', learnt to tithe (regularly) and enrolled in the 'Advanced Bible Class for Beginners'.

Any John would know this—especially any Baptist!

John missed all that Jesus was doing for Levi. John was looking at his own reactions. He was guided by his own concepts. He missed God's work because he was looking at human standards.

Jesus said to Levi, 'Here, try on this new name: Matthew,

"Gift of God".' John argued with himself: '"Gift of God"? The only "gifts" Levi ever received were bribes. Surely Jesus must have known what he did for a living. Surely the Messiah would not set such a precedent.' Levi, however, had just been the unworthy recipient of God's work. He was given his life back, and his name, ruined by all he had been connected with, was now changed. If Levi had been a woman, Jesus would have given him the name 'Grace'.

Grace is so often overlooked where judgment is concerned. Judgment looks at what we do and sentences us. Grace applies itself to who we are and helps us to be accountable and responsible. This is what John missed.

But that wasn't all. Jesus had said to Levi, 'Follow me,' but Levi had replied, 'No, Lord—you follow me!' John argued with himself again: 'Oh great! So now it is Jesus who does the following. He follows Levi to his house of sin to have dinner.' John was very worried about his own disciples being there. This was no place for Baptists. It was no place for God! But it seemed it was just the place for Jesus.

Then there was the issue of the leper. What if Andrew and Simon had caught the disease? That was very reckless (we can't have reckless Messiahs). To make it all worse, Jesus pardoned sins without a baptism and had started to fraternise with the Roman enemy. It was all too much.

Can you see the contradictions? If you can't, John could!

And that is the point.

It shows us that Jesus was not who John was looking for. He was not who the scribes and the faithful, godly Pharisees were looking for. And if we have the courage to be honest, he may not be entirely who we are expecting either. He did not conform to our morality then and he still doesn't. He still takes our morality and shows us that we are all guilty of the very things we judge. He then has mercy on *all* of us, embracing *all* with a life that refused to die at our hands.

If we need to identify our sins, all we have to do is see the greatest sin of humankind written in scars on his hands. What do these scars say? 'You are not who we were expecting.'

John said to Jesus, 'Should we keep looking?' Behind that question is a darker one: 'If so, then just who are you?'

It would be easy to stop here, but there is more. Jesus could have condemned John. He could have judged and humiliated his shortsightedness. But he didn't.

There is a lovely story in John 3, when the Baptist was still strong, full of faith and promise. Some of his disciples were apparently jealous that Jesus' ministry was increasing at the cost of John's, but he leapt to Jesus' defence.

'Pastor John, Jesus has come and he's "poaching" our disciples. Isn't that a little unethical? Surely the Messiah would know that a new church must receive permission from the movement before it "moves" into the district?'

Read John's defence of Jesus. The heading in the Bible I am using puts it this way: 'John the Baptist Exalts Christ'.

> 'You yourselves bear me witness, that I said, "I am not the Christ," but, "I have been sent before Him." He who has the bride is the bridegroom; but the friend of the bridegroom, who stands and hears him, rejoices greatly because of the bridegroom's voice. Therefore this joy of mine is fulfilled. He must increase, but I must decrease.
>
> 'He who comes from above is above all; he who is of the earth is earthly and speaks of the earth. He who comes from heaven is above all. And what he has seen and heard, that He testifies; and no one receives His testimony. He who has received His testimony has certified that God is true. For He whom God has sent speaks the words of God, for God does not give the Spirit by measure.
>
> 'The Father loves the Son and has given all things into His hand. *He who believes in the Son has everlasting life; and he*

who does not believe the Son shall not see life, but the wrath of God abides on him.'

What does this magnificent statement say to John himself as he sits alone with his doubts and fears in his prison cell? John disqualified himself by his own words!

But look at Jesus. How did he react? How did he deal with John's faithlessness, doubt and fear? Did he say, 'Get out your Bible, John, and look up what you said in John 3:22–36. Where does that put you now?' No. He sent an affirming message of inclusion back to the imprisoned prophet, via the mouths of the very ones who brought John's fears and doubts.

> 'The blind see and the lame walk; the lepers are cleansed and the deaf hear; the dead are raised up and the poor have the gospel preached to them. And blessed is he who is not offended because of Me.'

'John, the hopes of the nation, the words of the prophets and the answers to your prayers have all come to pass. Look and rejoice! If you can see past your fears, your questions and your doubts, recognising that God is at work, then you will see God in me. He will rise above what you wanted to see! However, if you look for what you wanted to see, you will only see what is not there, and you will miss God. What you want has become more important to you than seeing the truth.'

The challenge for all who look for God in Jesus is this: if you are going to be offended, don't be offended by Jesus. Be offended by your presumptions.

We presume that we know the truth and so we inflict it on everyone who comes into contact with us. We may preach 'confidence', but all we produce is 'fear'. John shows us that even he had doubts that overwhelmed his faith. John, who baptised Jesus, who saw the Spirit of God descending, who heard the voice of God affirming—if John could come to a point where everything he had seen was not enough, surely we can open our hearts to Jesus and let him help us with all that we secretly struggle with. When we are able to trust Jesus with our unbelief, he can help us find the truth. This is what he did for John.

John had to unlearn what he knew so that he could learn what Jesus was showing him. There is no other way, because it is our knowledge that obscures Christ.

In this uncertain journey of unlearning we don't abandon hope. We throw ourselves on his hope. We trust that in 'knocking, asking and seeking', *he* will 'open, answer and find' *us*, meeting our doubts with his answers. He did this for John. John was honest enough to admit it, honest enough to ask.

As we look at so many others who followed Jesus, we find this honesty was sadly lacking. Why was that sad? Because they had to wait for the consequences of their false expectations to overtake them before the truth finally came to light. Only then did they receive the comfort of Jesus for their fears that had always been there. Look at Peter—his life is a continual illustration.

The trouble is we want to 'see' straight away. We want 'instant faith'. We are scared of missing what everyone else 'sees' and experiences. We try so hard to cover our confusion and doubts. Because we have been taught that God responds to our faith, we presume he rejects our unbelief. So we deny it, hide it from ourselves, hide it from others and hope that God is not looking. We live in the fear that God is hiding around the corner and one day will simply kick our frail faith out of the kingdom.

What have we done to each other? What have we done as we proclaim our 'faith walk', talk our 'faith talk', sing our 'faith songs'—yet hide everything about us that screams 'Hypocrite!'? The secret contradictions are hidden deep inside our hearts.

Jesus, who held the faithless heart of John in his gracious hands, speaks to our doubts through his love for the broken

> **Jesus comes to us *because* we are faithless, hopeless, broken and flawed.**

Baptiser. Can we, once and for all, recognise that Jesus comes to us *because* we are faithless, hopeless, broken and flawed? He offers us his life because our life has failed.

When we are so hard on ourselves, we must remember that it was God who personally willed this prophet to be born. God chose this man, full of doubts and fears, to point the way to the Messiah he was not even expecting.

John's faithlessness 'prepared the way'!

John died believing, not because he had overcome his doubts and fears, but because Jesus had overcome them for him. Can you see it? Jesus comes to your doubts. Open them and he will reveal himself in the very things that you are fighting.

I remember a conversation I had over four years ago in what now seems like a different life. I was just starting out on the long road that has led me to where I am now, overwhelmed by God's answer to my brokenness and pain. A friend was comforting me and he simply said, 'You will find God in your fears.'

John did.

Can we?

10

Peter

'Who do you say that I am?'

I can still remember my first 'railway station romance'. Do you recall the days when all the school kids hung out at the railway station trying to impress each other? As a teenager I was part of the 'Killara Railway Station Mob'. Most of us attended the youth group at the local Anglican church, St Martins, Killara. The church, the station and most of the suburb seemed as if it had been transplanted from the English countryside into the oven of Australian summer heat. The buildings were covered with a respectable layer of ivy. The station was renowned for its gardens. The school children wore suits, blazers, ties and straw boaters. The girls were decked out in tartans and gloves. We were a page taken straight out of *Town and Country*. This was upper middle-class Australia in 1971.

We were locked in a '50s time-warp. Only the cars had changed. The Queen was still a welcome guest; her portrait hung in every public office. 'Hippies' were a strange phenomena found only in dark, decadent streets somewhere else.

Every morning and every afternoon, we would gather on the pavement next to the bus stop on the western side of the station. Why the western side, you ask? I'm not sure. It just happened to be 'the place'!

I learnt to flirt on the western side of Killara Station. I learnt to smoke without vomiting, going green, losing my balance or losing my practised air of 'coolness'. Smoking was the big thing. It was the greatest sin that a suit, tie, blazer and boater man could do. It was exciting, decadent, risky and rebellious, especially when the girls would strip their gloves from their manicured hands and inhale confidently. We would buy a packet of cigarettes, ensuring they were sitting in our shirt pocket as we loosened our ties (another dangerous act), removed our blazers and tilted our boaters. The girls would gather around us fussing and fawning, desperate for a date!

Dreamer!

We were the desperates. I was fifteen. I wore black horn-rimmed glasses—thick frames strong enough to support lenses that were cast-offs from the NASA space program. This apparatus perched unsteadily on my spotty nose, which I wrinkled continually to keep my goggles from falling from their orbit around my short-back-and-sides head. My equally spotty friends and I, with our double-pitched voices and our gangly arms and legs, were desperate to be 'known'. We were desperate to become the men that our bodies hinted at.

Every morning and every afternoon I would faithfully attend this ritual, hoping beyond hope that my beloved would notice who I was. Fortunately we had some help from her matchmaking friends and they brought about the revelation for us both. We eloped to a matinee session of *Love Story*—yes, it was a long time ago—and broke up after I failed in my attempts to be Ryan O'Neil, complete with pipe (I kid you not!). I am amazed that everyone didn't fall about laughing. To be honest, I think I scared the poor girl away!

Life is like that. As my generation grew into adulthood it became increasingly obsessed with image and 'self-improvement'. Nowadays analysis is trendy, psychiatrists' business cards are passed around the party set, plastic surgeons have magazines, and everyone wants to be everyone else. The Sunday magazines are full of advice to those who want to change their life, change their diet, change their shape. Food styles, hair styles, fashion trends, political trends, all are in a state of flux.

And yet our souls seem to be further away from understanding who we really are. We avoid responsibility to anyone less fortunate than ourselves, blaming the unemployed for their predicament and congratulating ourselves on our share portfolio. We look for leaders to show us the way and then vote them out of office when the way they lead is the wrong way. We dismiss any answers if they become too hard, too costly, too inconvenient, too political or too plain boring.

I failed at the western side of Killara station because, in searching for significance, I failed to recognise who I was. I searched high and low to become someone else.

I graduated from the railway station and continued my search throughout my teens and early adult years. I was looking without ever confronting the real question, 'who am I?' I simply wanted to find out 'who I wanted to be'.

Jesus knew who he was. He would have been strangely out of place at Killara station because he was not a desperate. He didn't need the affirmation of the other 'wannabes'. He wasn't struggling with his own image or the image that others had for him. Whether we like it or not, Jesus wouldn't have needed us to prop up his self-esteem.

Jesus' disciples, however, are instantly recognisable!

As we journey with this band of misfit missionaries, listening to their questions, watching their reactions and hearing their requests, it could be easy to judge. It could be easy to ask Jesus, 'Why these guys?' I believe that these twelve may have been selected because they represent *us*—our fears, our reactions and our expectations. As we look at these men grappling with the identity of Jesus and his impact on their lives, we can see ourselves. Perhaps it is this quality in the disciples that becomes the whole point of the exercise. We have often thought of them as our 'role models' and wanted to be 'made in their image'.

Perhaps it is a greater comfort to realise that they are made in ours.

Scattered throughout all four Gospels are gems of identifiable thickheadedness.

Jesus was transfigured on the top of a mountain. If you ever go to Israel, all the guides have their own theory as to which mountain it was. We travelled one day to the Golan Heights, a much fought over piece of high ground on the western side of the Sea of Galilee. We stood in a former Israeli military outpost and looked out over Syria. The camp site, although no longer in use, had obviously been highly fortified. In the distance on one side was the road to Damascus, and on the other side was the United Nations base. Our guide then pointed to a mountain north of us. That is the Mount of Transfiguration, he said.

We all looked and saw what was indeed a real mountain. A high, snow-capped mountain. I don't know about you, but before I visited the Golan Heights for some reason I saw in my mind a small hill and a little walk to the top. This was no small hill and it was not a short climb. It would have taken them days and involved 'real' climbing. We can only guess the content of the breathless conversations between Peter, James and John as they climbed up over rocks, cliffs and ledges, through the snow line to the summit. Here we have three fishermen climbing a mountain with a carpenter! They must have looked ridiculously out of place. Somehow I can imagine Jesus leading the way and the other three following behind. Jesus must have encouraged them on, but what were they saying in reply?

'What are we doing here? Where are we going? Why?'

Have you ever taken small children for a walk when they simply don't want to go? Every three minutes they stop and have a little grumble. You exercise parental patience, which is usually accompanied by some kind of bribe. Sometimes the bribe becomes a threat. Soon a nice walk deteriorates into a nightmare.

Jesus took his burly fishermen disciples for a climb, and from their perspective it must have been one of the craziest things they had ever done with him. We know the story, so we can wait excitedly for the miracle that awaited them. They had no such foresight. They climbed on in perplexed confusion, stifling their frustration, wondering what was ahead.

We need to understand that these situations with Jesus happened to a group of very ordinary men. When we remove the haloes from their heads and the 'St's' from their names, we can better understand what Jesus is showing us through them. If we turn them into super-spiritual saints, we miss the ordinary things that showed them who Jesus was. It was Jesus' reactions to their ordinary, everyday lives that show us the accessibility of God. God did not choose twelve powerful, faithful, prophetic men to lead the way for us. He chose twelve ding-a-lings to walk with us, sharing our perplexities and agreeing with our confusions. These twelve men show us a Christ who would choose you and me.

> **God did not choose twelve powerful, faithful, prophetic men. He chose twelve ding-a-lings.**

After what could easily have been days of climbing, the three disciples finally arrived with Jesus at the summit. They barely appear to have had time to draw breath!

> And He was transfigured before them. His face shone like the sun, and His clothes became as white as the light. And behold, Moses and Elijah appeared to them, talking with Him.

Peter looked around. Now this was more like it! Now he understood why Jesus had brought them there, even though it was a long climb and it would have been much better if the other guys could have seen this as well. I wonder if Peter also asked himself the question, 'Why hasn't Jesus done this before when there was a real crowd and real opposition?' How Peter would have loved to see the look on the Pharisees' faces, his friends' faces, their families' faces, even the face of his old boss, Zebedee. Then they would believe. Then they would say, 'Well done, Pete, we knew you were on a winner.' This finally had the 'spin' their campaign badly needed. Now all he had to do was organise a way for Capernaum, Galilee and even Jerusalem to see it. Then their cause could really get into high gear!

Have you heard a favorite expression of evangelists when they discover a great sermon illustration? It applies perfectly: 'This will preach!'

Peter put his mouth into fifth gear and blurted out:

> 'Lord, it is good for us to be here; if You wish, let us make here three tabernacles: one for You, one for Moses, and one for Elijah.'

What was in Peter's mind? Did he feel that at last he had a real role that would affirm him? Did he now have a job to do that would advance the kingdom of his ambition? Did he see the possibility of a new movement being birthed here on the mountain top? Were Peter's words really about his own search for identity and significance?

'Let's set up a camp for the three of you! You can stay here in your tents and I'll do the rest.'

Yes, access was poor, but look at the attractions. Jesus had at last graduated from being the suspect, miracle-working, Pharisee-insulting, law-breaking carpenter from Nazareth. He was shining like a glowworm! Look at his friends! No matter how many scribes and Pharisees had been insulted, no matter how many had questioned Jesus in the past, surely the sight of Moses and Elijah would add much needed credibility to their campaign. If Peter lived in our own time, he would have thought of a range of Bible studies entitled 'Climbing Your

Own Personal Mount of Transfiguration'. He would have already been designing T-shirts emblazoned with 'Three Amigos on the Mountain'. Peter could easily have been caught up in all that he and his mates could do to help Jesus along the way—and gain their own identity in the process.

His words, however, were cut short by God himself—something which I imagine would have been the ultimate humiliation:

When we approach Jesus trying to earn his approval, we forget just how loved we really are.

> While he was still speaking, behold, a bright cloud overshadowed them; and suddenly a voice came out of the cloud, saying, 'This is My beloved Son, in whom I am well pleased. Hear Him!'

Could this also be interpreted as: 'Peter, shut up and listen to my Son'?

Peter closed his eyes, swallowed his humiliation, took his swollen foot out of his mouth and wished he would learn to think before he spoke. He so wanted to be part of the action. He so wanted to be approved. He needed Jesus to know just how far he would go to help and support the mission. His heart needed to be affirmed, so he tried so hard to do everything he should so that now and again Jesus could simply say, 'Well done, Pete.'

I can so identify with this. Perhaps you can too. The sad truth is that when we approach Jesus trying to earn his approval, we forget just how loved we really are. Peter was going to learn the hard way, and it was going to hurt him more than anything else he had ever known. He was going to break his own heart, but in the process he was going to discover the heart of God.

Peter opened his eyes and saw no one but Jesus. He stifled the question, 'Did Moses and Elijah notice what a fool I made of myself?' He determined to make amends. He would try harder. He would succeed. He would become the man of God that Jesus must really want him to be.

Meanwhile, far below in the valley were the others. Alone. Waiting. Wondering. What were they discussing while the master was away?

'What on earth is Jesus doing now, and why aren't we included? What's so special about those three?'

You don't need much imagination to be able to hear the tone of jealousy and rejection. How many theories would have been tossed around at gatherings like this, as each disciple presented their own ideas as to what Jesus was up to and their role in it? These disciples had great plans, and I'm sure they were waiting for Jesus to make it all happen. They had all worked hard in the cause, leaving their families, friends, businesses and incomes. They had seen so much and they were expecting so much more—and in between the excitement, confusion and disappointment, they still dreamed of Jesus' kingdom and their own roles as leaders and ambassadors. But while Jesus, Peter, James and John had gone mountain climbing, they were sitting around, twiddling their thumbs.

Have you ever been part of a team brainstorming the future? As each person talks, the rest listen, hearing one by one the dreams and aspirations of their teammates. In these meetings many layers of leadership develop. Decisions are made and spokespeople are appointed. It would be naive to think that these nine men at the bottom of the mountain were any different. We must remember that these were ordinary men. I wonder what they decided to say to Peter, James and John when they returned with Jesus? What were the thoughts and plans that help us understand their final week in Jerusalem? What tensions were building in their hearts that would eventually lead to the actions of Judas and the betrayal of Peter? Actions that may well have been mirrored in the hearts of the others as they dealt with the end of their dreams.

Perhaps this explains a conversation they were having some time later on the way to Capernaum. Jesus asked them, 'What was it you disputed among yourselves on the road?' Finally they admitted that they were discussing who among them would be the greatest. Peter, James and John, after all they had seen and heard, still joined in this argument, which had probably been brewing for days. Can you imagine the embarrassment of these twelve men and the frustration of Jesus when they coyly admitted what they were talking about?

I wonder what went through Peter's mind as, yet again, he and his fellow disciples appear to blow it?

We can see their misunderstandings. *We* can see their answers coming because we know the end of their story. But if we can begin to see ourselves, our doubts and fears, in these men, we can join in their wonderment as the love of God in Jesus gradually unfolds before their eyes. The most wonderful revelation of all is that this love comes to their mistakes and not their triumphs.

> When Jesus came to the region of Caesarea Philippi, He asked His disciples, saying,
> 'Who do men say that I, the Son of Man, am?' So they said, 'Some say John the Baptist, some Elijah, and others Jeremiah or one of the prophets.'

Look at their answer: 'Some say John the Baptist, some Elijah, and others Jeremiah or one of the prophets.'

None say 'the Son of God, the Christ, the Messiah'.

According to a time-line of their ministry, by this stage they had been together for almost two years. So much had happened. Jesus had been baptised by John in the Jordan, with God's voice affirming him as it echoed across the river. He had called his disciples, and together they had traversed the countryside as Jesus healed the sick and raised the dead. They had watched as Jesus came into their own home town for all their family and friends to see (and how they would have longed for those closest to them to understand and believe as they did). He had preached words that brought hope to the hopeless. He had taught the multitudes with simple parables that defined God as one who includes the excluded, accepts the rejected, loves the unlovable, forgives the unforgiveable and holds the judges accountable. Jesus had crossed social and religious boundaries, breaking Levitical laws so that no one would see the back of God and be turned away from his love. He had fed five thousand on one occasion and four thousand on another. The disciples had seen these miracles happen, right before their eyes. He had walked on water, calmed the storm, opened blind eyes, unstopped the mouths of the mute.

And still the multitudes didn't see.

Effectively Jesus was asking his disciples, 'Am I succeeding in my mission?' And that mission was bound up with the question 'who am I?' But the multitudes had missed God in their midst. They were still looking for someone else.

To this point, while so many had been touched, so few had believed. How would you feel if two years of continual sacrifice yielded so little fruit? Did the disciples stop to think of these issues as together they admit to the Son of God that, up till now, this wonderful mission from heaven had failed?

Jesus had only one more question. What was going through the Son of God's mind as he looked back and saw only healed bodies? He had repaired the wineskins, but they hadn't changed the wine. The core of the mission was an inward revelation; the fruit was outward healing and change. He had the fruit, but the core, it seemed, remained unrealised.

So what was left? He had twelve men. What did they think?

Jesus now asked his disciples, 'But who do *you* say that I am?'

Did they know? Did they understand? Had they seen?

I hear this question coming from two places. First, I hear the voice of the Father, asking through the mouth of his Son, 'Am I Jesus?'

'Do you understand? Will you end your search? Will you stop seeking your proofs? Is Jesus enough to prove my reality? Can you finally let go of your expectations and have your concepts totally redefined in Jesus, my Son, my image? Will he be all that you are looking for? Are you able to step away from the multitudes? Are you any different?'

God the Father had initiated this great mission to humankind. He had travelled out of his eternity in the flesh of Jesus to reveal his true identity. Now the voice that could shatter the earth spoke with the solitary voice of his Son, crying, 'Can you see me?' Here is God at his most vulnerable, asking humanity, 'Who am I?' God silenced his power and majesty, turned down the light of his presence, reduced the roar of his voice to a human whisper, and asked twelve men, 'Am I Jesus?'

Second, I hear the voice of Jesus, the carpenter from Nazareth, carrying his Father's mission—a mission that was continually questioned and challenged, always at the mercy of expectation and misinterpretation. Jesus looked at his friends, twelve men who had had the closest encounter of the God kind that humanity will ever have this side of eternity, and wondered, 'They have seen me, but do they know me? Do they know who I really am?'

God the Father asked, 'Am I Jesus'? Jesus the Son asked, 'Am I God?'

This is everything. This is the whole gospel. There is no greater question, for it answers every other challenge. This question compels all to find their own answer—either to look again at their interpretations, or to step out in faith and allow Jesus to redefine everything they ever thought about God.

For almost two years, God pointed to the life of his Son to say, 'Here I am. This is who I am.' The only work that Jesus had to accomplish was revealing his Father. Everything else was secondary. Every day he revealed God to his disciples in simple acts of sacrificial love. But had they seen? Had they noticed? Had they felt the pain of the leper and then understood the enormity of his healing? Had they noticed the sacrifice of the centurion and then understood the love of God? Had they sat on the mountainside during Jesus' sermon and simply taken notes, or had they 'heard' and 'seen' the words that forever changed the concepts of God for those who until now were spiritual rejects?

> **The only work that Jesus had to accomplish was revealing his Father.**

Had they begun the process of unlearning? Or were they simply waiting for Jesus to do the 'God things' that promised them power and authority?

Did they believe?

Their answer must go to the very heart of humanity's worship: what then does God require of me?

If heaven could hold its breath, it was doing so now. Silent, paused in eternity, it looked on as the truth was finally being addressed. It was out in the open. All that had been said and done was now reduced to seven simple words: 'Who do you say that I am?'

Simon Peter answered and said, 'You are the Christ, the Son of the living God.'

Did all heaven shout for joy at that instant? Did the angels and elders break into singing and dancing? Did God himself rise from his throne with tears in his eyes and pronounce, 'It is finished'?

No.

The trip from the Golan Heights to Caesarea Philippi was steep. The narrow road descended, winding around barren hills, levelling out as it passed through small towns. Along the road were the ruins of Syrian army camps destroyed by the Israeli army in the Six Day War.

We travelled for an hour or so until at the bottom of the last hill we turned into what was obviously another tourist spot. It is easy to recognise these places because they are full of buses that dwarf the country roads, making their way from holy site to tourist stop, carrying their expectant cargo of pilgrims.

As always our guide shouted instructions. We were to gather in a small garden beside a stream where I would attempt to inspire our travel-weary friends. I grabbed my Bible and stayed behind with the guide. He was a young Jewish believer in Jesus who had been enchanting us with his stories and his faith. He had recently been discharged from the army where he served in Jericho.

'Where are we?' I asked him.

Again, as in Nazareth, his answer stopped me in my tracks.

'We are at the ruins of an ancient pagan temple that was built into the hillside surrounding a huge cave. A subterranean river runs through this cave, emerging at the garden where we are about to meet. This temple was a centre for pagan worship. Thousands of innocent children and young virgin girls were sacrificed here to appease the gods. According to accepted tradition, this is where Jesus asked his disciples, "Who do you say that I am?" It is called "the Gates of Hell".'

Can you see what I saw?

Jesus brought his disciples to this accursed place. As Jews, they were standing on unclean soil. Perhaps they looked around and secretly hoped that no one would see them.

Jesus pointed to the ruins, ruins that spoke volumes about who humanity thought God to be. These ruins were a worship manual concerning what the god of this temple required from the worshipper who sought blessing and favour. The temple would have run red with the blood of those who were sacrificed according to the laws and precepts of their bloodthirsty, vengeful god.

These ruins were humanity's response to the question that God the Father had asked through Jesus: 'Who do you say that I am?'

At the heart of this temple worship was the mistaken requirement that God would 'do this' if the worshipper 'did that'. What the worshipper did varied from small, simple favours that God blessed to horrid murderous sacrifices, but the intent and expectation remained the same. This was a God who required our actions *before* he performed his.

This is a common perception of God. It has its extreme in this temple site, but its philosophy stretches throughout time to all who seek to be blessed according to their actions. This temple, and all the 'temples' that have followed, say to the worshipper: 'Give more, pray harder, bring a greater sacrifice. If God is not answering your prayers, then you must work, work, work at your "worship".' What is this 'worship'? It is anything from the horrid hell of child sacrifice to the simple acts that ask God to respond. When we 'worship' this way, we are forever locked into performances that have to be increasingly pure, increasingly disciplined and increasingly presented. God's favour is presumed to be conditional, and we are locked into fear of doing anything that would cause his rejection. We fall into the trap of examining everything we do just in case we are not measuring up. We pray, study, give, work and exhaust ourselves because we are afraid to stop. We are afraid of rejection. We are scared of God.

Jesus came to this temple, the tragic exaggeration of this 'blessings and cursings formula', and simply asked, 'Is this necessary?'

If the disciples had seen who he really was, then they had seen for themselves what God requires of his worshippers. It certainly isn't this temple. Could they see that the truth must extend beyond this temple to the fundamental principles of humanity's need of acceptance?

Peter's answer sealed the truth. Every pagan temple, every guilt-stricken worshipper, every work and sacrifice, was now rendered obsolete and unnecessary.

'You are the Christ the Son of the living God.'

You are the embodiment of all that God is, does and requires.

Jesus stood outside this temple dedicated to the 'if you do this, I will do that' doctrine and affirmed Peter's revelation:

> 'Blessed are you, Simon Bar-Jonah, for flesh and blood has not revealed this to you, but my Father who is in heaven. And I also say to you that you are Peter, and on this rock I will build My church, and the gates of Hades [hell] shall not prevail against it.'

Suddenly, as I stood in the car park surrounded by tourist buses, I saw the most wonderful truth. As the disciples looked up at the huge rock looming above them, with its ruins and its cave of sacrifice, Jesus was saying to them:

'The rock on which I will build my kingdom is not the rock of your sacrifices, works and deeds. It is the rock of who the Messiah is, what he does and what he requires. It is not about what you do; it is about what I will do. When that is understood, then this place and all the other conditional "gates of hell" will never again torment worshippers with the guilt and insufficiency of what they do and cannot do.'

I looked up at the ruins of this temple and realised that the 'gates of hell' only admitted those who came carrying their own sacrifices. These were cruel gates that demanded worship, sacrifice, standards and fear. These gates fall when Jesus' church

> **Jesus had to prove that his love was beyond humankind's capacity to earn it.**

opens its doors to admit all who come—those on the 'inside' as well as those 'outside'. All the flawed and failed sons and daughters of the kingdom. We all come with this free ticket—a ticket that we can never afford. A ticket that is bought by grace and received by faith.

This is the church that Jesus came to build. This is the kingdom that he preached. 'His will done on earth as it is in heaven.' This church is a rock that disarms the works we do to seek the approval of God and people. This church heals us from the anxieties of unfulfilled works and sacrifices, showing us a God who will never turn us away, no matter what we do or don't do.

To build this church, Jesus must tell his disciples about the cross, and they must come to the place where they fully understand it.

> From that time Jesus began to show His disciples that He must go to Jerusalem, and suffer many things from the elders and chief priests and scribes, and be killed, and be raised on the third day.

The only way that Jesus could convince this world of the enormity of his love was to prove it in such an unconditional way that all who believed in him could never return to the 'gates of hell'. Human beings had to be released from their conditional religious 'wages'. There was only one way to do this. Jesus had to prove that his love was beyond humankind's capacity to earn it.

It is here that an amazing convergence unfolds between what Israel desired and what God had planned.

Israel was looking for the Messiah, and they knew who they were looking for. They were confident that God would bless or curse according to works, deeds and sacrifices, and because of this, Israel knew what this God required for blessing and prosperity. The law was full of the correct commandments and the appropriate judgments. Their worship centred on the maintenance of their righteousness according to the law.

This law, however, excluded and condemned Jesus. To use their own words, it revealed him as a lawbreaker, a drunkard and a glutton. From their perspective, there was only one solution for the problem of Jesus, and that was his death. The elders, the scribes, the Pharisees and the high priest himself had no other way. Either Jesus was God and they resigned, or he was a blasphemer and was put to death.

Jesus, on the other hand, *was* the Messiah, though Israel failed to recognise him. His mission was to reveal, for all time, to all worshippers, who his Father really was and what he really required. How could he walk against the tide of broken expectations and prove his Father's love? The only way was to submit to the worst that humankind could do. Only then would God be understood as the One who refuses to turn from unconditionality to conditionality, no matter what the provocation.

Now the fallen heart of humankind is finally revealed. We are unforgivable, irredeemable, unjustifiable and totally devoid of morality. God's forgiveness is unconditionally extended towards the worst of us.

Now we see his glory.

The 'gates of hell' crumble and fall.

Only one thing defeats the pagan temple at Caesarea Philippi, and it is the absolute insufficiency of anything that humanity can do to gain God's favour. The cross has sentenced the earth to judgment. God has atoned for and forgiven humanity's greatest sin, and now the grace that we live in, the grace that destroys the 'gates of hell', the grace that constantly atones for our absolute unworthiness, is unconditional, unmerited and free.

It is at this point that our temples of sacrifice and conditionality become unnecessary.

Then and only then can our works of love, our 'worship', be free. We can never impress God, never be worthy to receive the blessings, never righteous enough to atone for our sins. We can only be grateful enough to respond with love. This response echoes the love of Jesus as he continues to enter the dark places, the loveless places, the hidden and rejected places, to bring his love, light and acceptance.

Our 'worship' is to respond to our world as he responded to us.

Peter, the Galilean fisherman, full of the affirmation of his confession, now had an enormous challenge. The revelation must change his expectations.

But Peter missed it. As Jesus explained the suffering that lay in front of him, Peter cried out, 'God forbid! No way! Not while I'm around!'

This proved that Peter never really 'got it' in the first place. If he had, he would have known that there was no other way. For the true identity of Jesus is forever proved and revealed at the cross.

Jesus rebuked Peter:

> 'Get behind Me, Satan! You are an offence to me, for you are not mindful of the things of God, but the things of men.'

Jesus took this proud fisherman, so eager to please, and said to him, 'You devil!' Peter must have been crushed.

For two years he had sought the approval of Jesus. He had left his boat, his nets, his mates and his work. He had left his home, his wife and his family. He had forsaken all to follow

Jesus. He had walked the roads of Judea and Galilee, doing his best to earn Jesus' respect. He had made some humiliating mistakes and tried so hard to get it right. Now here in Caesarea Philippi, his dream finally materialised. He finally got to say the right thing at the right time, and Jesus said, 'Well done, Peter.' He could now lift his head from his insecurity and see the smile on Jesus' face. And his friends were there to see his finest moment.

But it only took a few words from Jesus before Peter again opened his mouth. He couldn't help it. His heart leapt to protect his master. He would not permit anyone to take Jesus away from him. Jesus was destined for greatness. Peter knew it, always had. He was going to make sure of it. He would fight for his master until he was crowned king of Israel. Jesus would subdue his enemies under his feet, Israel would be delivered, the crowds would cheer and the kingdom would come. This was the hope of Israel. This was the hope of every Jewish son and daughter. Peter was here, alongside the 'captain of the armies of the Lord', and he was the 'captain's lieutenant'. It was only a small army, but they would be like Gideon. Together they would defeat Israel's enemies.

In Peter's eyes, Jesus' time, their time, the nation's time, had come.

'Jesus, I will never permit your defeat.'

Peter may just as well have said, 'I will stand in the way of your victory.'

With these words, Peter rebuked the work of God. He betrayed Jesus' mission. At the heart of his protest was the misinterpretation of who God really is. Peter's Jesus was the Son of *Peter's* God, not the living God. Jesus could never be subject to Peter's interpretations. Or anyone else's.

So despite the revelation of who Jesus was, Peter's expectations hadn't changed. He shows us just how close we can get and still miss the truth. Peter still had to leave behind his needs that centred around 'what Jesus could do for him, and what he could do for Jesus'.

Broken expectations. They would eventually put Jesus on the cross. But the miracle is that the very thing that would kill him would also finally prove the nature of God. Humankind's broken expectations would soon become nails, and then and only then would the question 'who am I?' be answered.

The very thing that would kill Jesus would also finally prove the nature of God.

As Jesus cries out, 'Father, forgive them,' we must come to grips with *what* he has forgiven.

This was the lesson that lay ahead for Peter and the disciples. There would be much more to forgive yet.

Peter climbed the Mount of Transfiguration and descended to the pagan temple at Caesarea Philippi. In both places he missed the truth of 'This is my beloved Son in whom I am well pleased.'

God announced that his pleasure was simply in his Son, nothing more, nothing less.

As I stood in the car park that had been built for all the tourists, I looked up again at the temple ruins, its huge cliff face and cave of sacrifice. Above this temple, obscured by the foothills, rose a mountain, its steep slopes climbing high into the clouds.

The temple of the 'Gates of Hell' was built into the foundations of the 'Mount of Transfiguration'!

11

Rich, Young and Upwardly Mobile

I had two dreams when I was a teenager. In my younger days I imagined myself as Ben Casey or Dr Kildare. If both of these names mean nothing to you, you must have been born some time after the late '60s. Ben Casey and Dr Kildare were TV medicos, long before Hawkeye Pearce of MASH or the ER team filled our screens with face masks. I would sit glued to the television watching these men as they healed the sick and spoke hope to the dying. I longed to join them one day as, gowned, scrubbed and gloved, I entered the world of the sick and turned it around—all in one black and white sixty-minute episode.

When I was a small impressionable boy, my family had a wonderful doctor. His name, believe it or not, was Dr Angel. I clearly remember our first encounter. I was five. I know this because I wasn't wearing glasses—my first five years were spent squinting at a softly out-of-focus world. One day, as I blindly groped around the fuzzy edges of my sandpit, I trod on a broken piece of roofing tile which was hiding in the sand, just waiting for a poor 'blind' boy to come along. (What it was doing there I don't know; the roof of our house was covered in aluminium!) I stepped on the tile and yelped. Okay, I tell a lie: I screamed. I screamed and screamed until the doctor, forty-five minutes later, removed the needle from my foot and the anaesthetic took hold. By that time everyone's ears were ringing from the noise. (For the sake of my self-esteem, please know that I am exaggerating just a little!)

The doctor took my battle-scarred foot in his wise and gentle hands and carefully sewed three stitches. I watched, awestruck, and immediately fell in love with his profession. I too wanted to save the world. Up to this time, I had been praying that God would make me Superman. Now I wanted to be 'Superdoc'.

As I grew, the dream stayed with me. All through my piano lessons, as I learnt the trumpet and the guitar, I was going to be 'Superdoc'. On the football field I knew the truth; I wasn't a footballer, I was a doctor. When my first day's footy practice ended, I went home trying to understand if being the '5/8th' was because I was small. My self-esteem progressed from bad to worse as I became the 'hooker'. The coach still yelled, 'Bullock, you're running the wrong way!' They didn't know that hidden under that voluminous football jumper (dress?) was 'Super-duperdoc'.

I grew into the jersey, and the dream grew with me. Ben Casey gave way to the brave medics on *Combat* and *Twelve O'Clock High*. I was destined—touched by 'an angel'!

Music, however, started to become a major influence. In 1969 I fell in love with another profession. The Beatles had just recorded *Abbey Road* and I was hooked. Piano took a back seat as the guitar provided an instant open door to the allure of Folk and Rock. I bought music books by the score (terrible pun!). I practised till my fingers were sore. And a new dream was born.

Throughout the first four years of high school, when I wasn't at Killara railway station, or glued to *Marcus Welby, MD*, these two dreams competed for my attention. I studied to fulfil both. 'Paging Dr Dylan. Dr Dylan, you are wanted in recovery.'

I turned seventeen in November 1972, a long way from Dr Angel's surgery and a long way from my first dream. It had been a turbulent year for me as my search for the answer to the question 'who am I?' intensified. The late '60s and early '70s were a time of intense social upheaval, and I was caught up in the excitement of challenging traditional concepts by breaking the mould of the establishment. I left the suit, tie, blazer and boater school and enrolled in an alternative.

It may have worked for some, but it absolutely failed for me. Strike out the doctor dream.

That left music. I finished school determined to become the next Paul McCartney.

I poured everything into my quest. I bought the best amp and the right bass guitar, a 'Hofner Beatle Bass'. I practised. I performed. I made the right connections and went to the best concerts. I played in band after band, blasting everyone within earshot with an eclectic brand of highly original noise. I moved out of home with a bunch of shaggy musicians into a 'rock-'n'roll house', and we practised all night, all week, all weekend. Across the road was one of Sydney's more significant churches, and while we took a break from our aural adventures, we watched the congregation arrive for the services that we were about to sonically invade with more chords than a hymn book. (Four years ago I met the minister, told him the story and watched his bemused expression as he put a face to his sermon interruptions.)

When you are in a band every move counts. The 'pop industry' is all about the right people, the right place, the right songs, the right opportunities, all taken advantage of at the right time. Every 'lead' is followed with missionary zeal. Every 'break' could be the big break. Every 'lead break' is honed to ear-dazzling perfection. You learn to take advantage of everything—and sadly, as the history of modern music shows us, everyone takes advantage of you.

The dream died every time we 'died' on stage, and that was often. I remember one night. Somehow we had wangled ourselves a gig in one of Sydney's best venues. We practised and practised and prepared ourselves for instant stardom. After our first set, a young teenage girl came up to the band. We prepared our egos for the adulation.

She simply wanted to know why we hadn't tuned our guitars.

I spent the best part of one year travelling in a 'kombi van' with six other musical misfits, playing up and down the east coast of New South Wales. I watched despairingly as my dream disintegrated. Every contact failed. Every opportunity ended as we reloaded the truck with the tons of gear that was owned by the bank. Every 'hit' was a 'miss'. Eventually the dream was just a memory, the songs were just rhythmic reminders of all that I had hoped would happen and the friends went home. In the end, it was the end.

Travelling with a bunch of headstrong guys, waiting for the promises, hopes and expectations to materialise. Blaming each other and the manager when all that was left was disappointment and disillusionment.

Andrew, Peter, James and John had such high hopes for Jesus. They were joined by other dreamers, other men who had heard the words 'Follow me'. Twelve men with twelve different concepts of 'the kingdom'. Twelve men with twelve separate interpretations of the word 'Messiah'. Twelve men who were hoping that this Jesus would propel the nation and them into revival, liberation, deliverance, prosperity, repentance, vindication, justification and all manner of national prominence. Twelve reactions to the uncertainties and inconsistencies of their journey as their personal dreams failed to be clothed with Jesus' flesh.

They watched opportunities come and go as influential men with influential friends came to see Jesus. So many times they must have said to each other, 'Look, God has opened a door for us.' So many times they must have struggled with their disappointment as Jesus appeared to miss the opportunity they were sure was 'of God'.

Those whom they were sure would be an asset to 'the way'

were pushed out of the way. Religious leaders were insulted. Levitical laws were broken in situations that in their eyes weren't worth the drama. Jesus seemed to go out of his way to reject the right people and accept the wrong. He made a mockery of their pursuit of righteousness by insisting they accompany him to the houses of sinners, tax collectors and publicans. He became increasingly antisocial as he befriended a prostitute. He made them stay for three days in a Samaritan town because of a well-side conversation with a many-times divorced Samaritan woman. Both these women were outcasts from their society, but Jesus simply expected the disciples to share his compassion. The nation was under cruel occupation and subject to harsh taxes, yet Jesus refused to shun the servants of this system. He befriended Israel's enemies, making a mockery of the nation's pain. He refused to take sides and reserved his most cutting words for those who dared point out these 'inconsistencies'.

The sad tragedy was that everything about Jesus was misinterpreted by the disciples and the multitudes. Every time the grace and love of God would descend from heaven, a 'living interpretation', they would instead choose to look into their broken interpretations and see failure. A failure that centred on Jesus.

Are these words too hard for you? Please, every time you feel that I am being unjustifiably unfair, remember judas's kiss, listen to the cockcrow, look at the cross, and take note of the rapidly disappearing backs of his disciples.

> Now a certain ruler asked Him, saying, 'Good Teacher, what shall I do to inherit eternal life?'
> So Jesus said to him, 'Why do you call Me good? No one is good but One, that is, God. You know the commandments: "Do not commit adultery," "Do not murder," "Do not steal," "Do not bear false witness," "Honour your father and mother."'

And he said, 'All these things I have kept from my youth.'

So when Jesus heard these things, He said to him, 'You still lack one thing. Sell all that you have and distribute to the poor, and you will have treasure in heaven; and come, follow Me.'

Whenever I used to read this, I felt a guilty fear of exclusion and failure. I couldn't work out what Jesus was saying. This guy seemed okay. He was obviously righteous. He was going through the same rituals that I was going through: keeping the law and seeking Jesus. When Jesus told him that this wasn't enough, I couldn't help it—I looked at my own life and knew that I could never fulfil what Jesus was demanding. I looked around at my colleagues and friends, and it was obvious from their confident, assured faces that I was the only one feeling guilty; so I wasn't living up even to their standards. This made it a whole lot worse. If I comforted myself by saying, 'Don't worry, Geoff, they aren't fulfilling what Jesus wants either', I felt worse still. Now we were all failures according to Jesus' standards, and what we were believing for had already been denied.

I tried to give more. I tried to do more. I felt increasingly worse.

What was in the heart of this rich young ruler as he sought out Jesus? Perhaps he had been on the treadmill for many years. He had become successful, affluent and influential. Everything on the outside looked great. His life was 'blessed'. His work prospered. He had every reason to feel satisfied. He attended church, obeyed all the rules, did all the right things.

But something was missing. Something wasn't right. On the outside, everyone wanted to be his friend. On the inside, he was missing something and longed for more.

He had heard of Jesus. Perhaps Jesus would show him what was missing. It was probably only a little thing. He had already fulfilled all the big things.

The rich young ruler came looking for the 'magic button',

the 'special prayer', the 'right work', the 'appropriate ministry'. He came asking what else he had to do. This is a dangerous question, because it presumes that everything already being done has been accepted.

Jesus said, 'Keep the commandments.'

The rich young ruler knew that this wasn't the problem because he was one of the good guys. But to be sure, he thought he should at least ask for clarification.

'Which commandments?'

Jesus reply wasn't groundbreaking. There wasn't any new revelation here. The rich young ruler knew all these and the others as well. He had faithfully kept them all, so this couldn't be the problem.

> **The rich young ruler came looking for the 'magic button', the 'special prayer', the 'right work'.**

What was missing?

It was important for this young man not to lose face. He did not want Jesus to think that his spiritual hunger had anything to do with spiritual poverty. That would never do. After all, he *was* blessed. He *had* prospered. What he really wanted was *more*. He was sitting at the top of his professional 'tree'. He had climbed the ladder of success, and now he wanted to crown all this with 'eternal security'. He was sure that this would silence the doubts he was hiding from everyone, especially this teacher, Jesus.

What was missing?

This man's life would fit so very comfortably into many of our churches. We would see him coming a mile off; the disciples probably did. His clothes would give him away as a man of money, influence, power. He would make a great 'deacon' or even (after some counselling) an 'elder'. He could sit on the 'financial board'. He certainly would be an asset, a 'gift from God'. Men like this are courted by all manner of causes. They have much to give and therefore find their way onto all manner of boards and committees. Yes, the benefits such a man can bring are obvious—so obvious that we would probably have chased after him.

Could an awareness of his own worth also have been part of the young man's motivation for seeking out Jesus? Jesus' cause needed help; the man needed assurance. They could enter into a 'win-win' arrangement. It is possible that the rich young ruler even thought he didn't need much help from Jesus. All he wanted was an answer so that he could go away and add it to all the other things he was doing. In return, he could be of even greater help to Jesus and his disciples than they could be to him.

The rich young ruler did not see his need. He was not aware of his total insufficiency.

Jesus, however, was not interested in what this man could do for him. Jesus was only interested in what he could do for this man. This was what was missing. The rich young ruler did not see his need. He was not aware of his total insufficiency.

This young man came to Jesus full of confidence. He may have lacked something, but he saw his lack in the context of all that he had. His confidence was firmly planted in what he had done and what he could do. Everything that he said echoed his confidence in his own ability to live, prosper and save himself. He was absolutely unaware of his insufficiency. He had mistakenly come to the conclusion that God had blessed his life as a result of what he had done. He did not realise that while God may have blessed, this was not in response to his supposed 'virtues'.

We must never presume that our blessings, whatever they may be, are 'earnings'. They are always 'gifts'.

Like the builder who put his foundations on sand, this young man came to the master architect and engineer saying, 'I need a final architectural statement for my building. I was thinking about a windvane. Tell me, Jesus, what would be the best model (at the right price, of course)? After all, this building will be here long after we're gone!'

But Jesus took one look at the foundations and said, 'Are you kidding? You've built on sand. How on earth can you be so foolishly confident? You don't need a windvane to crown your building. Your foundations will see to that! Pull it down before it falls on someone. Start again. Don't fool yourself—the building never proves the foundations.'

The issue was not riches. The issue was blind, arrogant, self-righteous confidence.

Jesus had always met people in their place of need, with nothing to lose and everything to gain. This young man was different. He didn't have needs. He had everything. He simply wanted more.

He came to Jesus firstly seeking to be recognised. He confidently proclaimed the righteousness of all he had done since he was a boy. It appeared as if he was waiting for Jesus to respond with a 'Well done! What a clever young ruler you are!'

Jesus ignored this man's 'righteousness'. He asked him to look further. Jesus pointed him to those who had nothing.

Why? Because all along Jesus had been saying, 'Blessed are the poor in spirit, for theirs is the kingdom of heaven.'

The only way for this young man to receive the eternal life that he sought was to become poor in spirit. He had to abandon his confidences, taste the reality of his sinfulness and, stricken with his unexpected guilt, come to Jesus for mercy.

Does this sound hard? Do we have to sell everything before we can receive the kingdom of heaven and enter into eternal life? The answer depends on your confidence. If you think that anything other than the grace and mercy of God will save you, then get rid of it. It is an obstacle. Your own confident self-righteousness will never bring your heart to a place where it will see Jesus and his kingdom. It will hinder you. It will harm you. It will trip you up and bring you down. In the process you will fight to protect your confidence at the expense of everything else. When this confidence starts to fail, you will sacrifice whatever is left to maintain it. Your heart and soul will be locked into the continual pursuit of everything that you think is necessary, and you will miss entirely the simple truth and revelation of all that Jesus has done for those who are 'poor in spirit'.

If you are 'rich in spirit', you will only see what you have earned. The 'poor in spirit' see what Jesus has given.

> **Jesus saw in the young man a spirituality so confident in its own works that it didn't need God at all.**

The young man had to leave behind the confidence he had in his own works. He had to come to Jesus to receive God's work on his behalf. He couldn't have both, although that was what he wanted. Grace does not flow from our good works like a windvane that crowns our edifices. Grace replaces our works.

But the rich young ruler couldn't leave behind all that had affirmed him. He couldn't turn away from all he had done, all he had presumed God responded to. This is the danger that lurks behind our spiritual pride. We ask Jesus to crown our righteousness. It is impossible.

Jesus gave this young man the only option he had. 'If you want eternal life place your confidence in nothing but me, then live a life that responds to grace with graciousness.'

This is not what the young man wanted. Perhaps Jesus was a total disappointment to him. He turned and walked away.

Jesus saw in the rich young ruler a spirituality that was dangerously godless—a spirituality so confident in its own works that it didn't really need God at all. God was only a back up, or a top up. He certainly wasn't this young man's life raft.

He had come to Jesus with everything to give and virtually nothing to receive. He left unwilling to give and unable to receive.

Jesus did not turn this man away. He made the choice himself. He chose to place his faith in his own abilities and walked away from all that Jesus offered. His sad and sorrowful rejection implied: 'I don't need what you have to give, for I already have everything I need.'

What a sad tragedy. He was unaware of his poverty. He walked away from life and chose instead to become an observer watching the decay of all that he thought was strong. He missed the truth because he could not accept what was wrong.

The poor could have been fed, but the rich young ruler walked away in his wealthy security, refusing to respond to their cries. His spirituality was bound up in the accumulation of the riches of blessings and the blessings of riches. He was the sole focus of all he did. His faith was directed at his own needs. His heart was hard to the needs of others. His spirituality absolved him from his responsibility to care.

Stand in the slums of Kenya in the shoes of this young man and look Jesus in the face. Now try to say, 'I have kept all the commandments since I was a child. What must I do to receive eternal life?' What must I do to receive without losing, gain without giving?

Our giving will never reveal our righteousness, for that is assured by God. Our giving, however, will reveal our gratitude. When we seek 'more of God', searching for 'greater experience' and a 'new touch', could we just pause long enough to hear the cry of an orphan? When we see a Saviour who gave everything away so that we could know his love, surely we can find the appropriate response, the 'worship' that reflects sacrifice—a selfless sacrifice that seeks to give because of the 'wealth' that has been received.

The rich young ruler walked away blind to all that he had been given and unaware of all that he could give.

What would we say if our small outreach church was struggling from service to service and this rich young ruler, confident, affluent, well-connected, came running up asking, 'Need anything? I want to be blessed. Pray for my salvation'? Would we sign him up, pray him up, wrap him up and yell 'Hallelujah! God has answered our prayers'? Or would we help him to become 'poor in spirit'?

The money wasn't important. The young man was.

This is what Jesus saw. Jesus had everything to give, but there was nothing he could do. The man's own works stood in the way. We can only offer what he has given us, and sadly, this rich young ruler wasn't even prepared to admit his need in order to receive. This is why he turned away.

What was going through the minds of the disciples as this valuable asset, this contact, this 'God-given opportunity', walked away in his sorrow?

> When Jesus saw that he became very sorrowful, he said, 'How hard it is for those who have riches [in self-confidence and self-sufficiency] to enter the kingdom of God!'

The disciples looked around perplexed and asked, 'Who then can be saved?'

Good question. After all, the young man seemed to be the 'right stuff'.

Jesus answered the question the only way he could. There are no favourites, no one deserving. No one is rewarded, for God will respond to only one thing. It isn't what the rich young ruler, Peter, James, John, Mother Teresa, St Francis, Billy Graham or you and I do that is rewarded. What we all do has been judged. God responds to Jesus alone, who took the sentence and burst out of the death that should be ours with a life that is now bestowed on us as a free gift.

> But Jesus looked at them and said, 'With men it is impossible, but not with God; for with God all things are possible.'

All things, even the unthinkable. God would forgive the planet of his executioners, saving them from the just consequences of their actions.

But the disciples still didn't get it. Jerusalem was calling Jesus as they watched the kingdom they were expecting slip from their grasp. Perhaps one of them arranged for this young man to come to Jesus, and now this 'God-given opportunity' had been insulted and sent away.

What could they do about it?

12

The Garden

There is a scene in the old black and white movie *Twelve O'Clock High*. An American bomber group is flying daylight raids over Germany. They are taking heavy losses and yet their mission continues. Their squadron leader takes their case to bomber command and pleads for a break in the campaign. His men are tired, many are wounded, many have died. The pressure of the heavy losses and constant fear is taking an enormous toll on these young men, the oldest barely out of his teens. Your heart goes out to this man. He is carrying his men on his weary shoulders and believes that his case must be heard.

Bomber command answers these complaints by dismissing the squadron leader and replacing him with a hard, demanding man who immediately begins to rule with a firm, unsympathetic hand. The tired squadron of shell-shocked men are confronted with renewed drills, withdrawn privileges and tightened discipline. They are informed in no uncertain terms that 'the mission is more important than the man'.

No surrender, no retreat. They take off again to suffer greater losses.

Now, you can rightly say that this was war, and war demands the highest sacrifices. History, regrettably, proves you right. The first twenty minutes of *Saving Private Ryan* will forever be burnt into my memory with images of young men sacrificing themselves for the hope that their flag would fly from their enemy's flagpole. Hollywood filmmaking at its best—yet it still failed dismally to show the reality that faced those young soldiers on the morning of D-Day, June 6, 1944.

This concept of noble sacrifice for higher goals pervades so many of our great quests and ambitions. Have you ever been in the team locker room before a Grand Final? The same language is used. There is a story of a young footballer who had fractured the vertebrae in his neck in a bone-snapping tackle. He was carried off the field, restrained by his coach and team doctor as he pleaded to be allowed back into the game.

Businesses grow at the expense of men and woman who can't keep up. The corporate ladder has no safety net. Littered around every company headquarters are the shattered lives of those who had to be sacrificed for the company's vision and share price. Economic rationalism, a politically correct word for 'greed', has stripped country towns of the simple services that city folk take for granted. No, I am wrong here. The city folk *demand* them from a government which was once for the people and by the people, but is now for the balance sheet and by the profit. If it works economically, it must be right. Yes, I know the principle that greater wealth creates wealth for all; but as I look around, I can't help observing that greater wealth creates greater greed and a growing gap between the 'haves' and the 'have nots'.

Once upon a time, cities were built around industries. The industries supported the town as the townsfolk worked together to support the industry. Now, as coal mines, steel mills, textile factories and all their associated industries close, it appears the town must carry the company until it can afford to restructure its workforce, reduce its costs, leave the town and its workers, and amalgamate with another company in another state or country. The mission of the 'board' is to please the shareholders, returning increased profits, higher share prices and greater dividends. The responsibility of the company to each worker, each man or woman, is left behind with its deserted buildings and decaying infrastructure. The town suffers as the company prospers.

At the core of our society is the selfish proposition that one man's mission, be he a Major-General, a General Manager or a Prime Minister, is more important than another man's welfare.

How can this conservative section of our society walk from church to boardroom without ever seeing the contradiction?

Jesus was alone in the garden. His disciples were sleeping the sleep of too much food and wine. He had come to the pinnacle of his work, the finest moment of all time. The world should have been awake, waiting in awestruck anticipation for what is about to happen between it and the God of the universe. But it was ignorant, and its sleeping sons were lying under the olive trees there in Gethsemane without an inkling of what was about to be declared to eternity.

Jesus and his disciples had just celebrated the Passover, a meal that was both a memorial and a prophetic statement. When we look at the conversations and politics of the twelve, though, it seems this last meal was more pathetic than prophetic. The gap between Jesus and his disciples appeared to be wider than ever before. By the end of this night, the secrets of their hearts would be opened for all to see. By the end of this night, life for twelve men would never be the same again.

The next few hours brought into clear relief the differences between reality and expectations. The disciples appeared to be restless, waiting for the 'finale' to begin. The events of that night are key to understanding who God is, what he does and what he expects.

Have you ever had your feet washed? I have—once. It was the most vulnerable thing that has ever happened to me. I had to submit myself to an act of love. Life is so often a reciprocal arrangement: 'You scratch my back and I'll scratch yours.' Foot washing is entirely different. There is nothing you can do in return. You sit, feet cradled in the hands of a 'servant' who has to kneel before you, closer to your smelly toes than you will ever be. You can't earn it, return it or share it. You can only receive it.

God has come to wash the feet of humanity! Words fail to express the absolute beauty and majesty of this act. God takes off his clothes, wraps himself in a clean towel, kneels before his fallen creatures with their hearts full of selfish ambition, and gently bathes their dirty feet, drying them carefully with the towel around his waist.

Peter's guilt would be forever seasoned by this simple act of unconditional, unmerited love.

Jesus came to Peter, who promptly shot his mouth off. 'Lord, surely you know that I'm in the business of serving you! I'm the one who needs your approval. I can't let you do this; it would humiliate me. I should wash your feet.'

Peter could not receive. He had to earn.

Jesus drew the line in the sand. 'Peter, this is the only way to see me, because this is who I am, what I have come to do, and therefore what you must do. Receive it, Peter. There is no other way.'

We all know what Peter did before the end of the night. Jesus ensured that Peter's ensuing guilt and shame would be forever seasoned by this simple act of unconditional and unmerited love. From then on, whenever the shame of a fireside betrayal haunted and accused this failed man, he remembered the hands of Jesus washing his faithless feet.

Jesus moved on to James and John. One by one he washed their feet.

Zebedee's boys. They had come a long way from their days as disciples of John the Baptist as well as from their boats, nets and servants on the shores of Galilee. However, it is clear that although they had left Galilee, Galilee had not left them.

Only a matter of weeks before, they arranged for their mother to come and ask Jesus if her sons could have positions of authority in the kingdom. 'Jesus, they're good boys. Let them sit on your right and left.' James, John and the wife of Zebedee had no real idea who Jesus was, even after three years of healings, miracles, even the transfiguration. Three years that saw God's love pouring out through this man to the most undeserving. They were still plotting and planning for their own goals, trying to bring about human kingdoms with themselves planted firmly on the thrones.

Now Jesus came to Simon the Zealot. Simon looked down at Jesus holding his feet, gently washing, patting them dry. Was Simon thinking of his anger when Jesus chose the faith of the Roman centurion over his? Simon's friends had been martyred and their deaths were crying out for justice. Jesus, how could you?

Next came Thomas. Thomas, who in less than a week would be so broken that he would not be able to summon the faith to believe. What would bring Thomas to this point? What disappointments would empty this disciple of all hope? Jesus held his disciple's feet in the palms that would become Thomas's final proof. Jesus and Thomas together looked at these hands as they lovingly gave their gift of love. Nothing had stopped these hands of grace and nothing would.

Jesus came to Judas and washed his feet. Beloved Judas, chosen Judas, privileged Judas. Poor, disappointed Judas. Judas's last memory of his Lord was the love on his face and the touch of his hands.

That night two disciples were joined by their broken dreams and disillusionment as Judas and Peter were united by the betrayal that was in both their hearts. Only Judas acted. Peter ran.

Jesus finished his work of love as his disciples got up to argue about who was the greatest among them. Then Jesus announced to his friends that one would betray him.

They appeared to be astonished, saying, 'Who, me?'

Please forgive me if I seem to draw a long bow here, but I wonder why they were incredulous? Was it because they were unaware or was there some other reason? Was it because each one in his heart had betrayed Jesus many times? Peter was about to. James and John's request for personal authority deserved the same rebuke that Peter received at Caesarea Philippi. Time and time again, these twelve men had questioned and challenged Jesus. Were they now doing it again?

Is it even possible that although Judas was the one to carry it out, he was not completely alone in his plan? I have been on committees that have plotted behind the chairman's back. Churches are full of them. Governments are overthrown by the secret words quietly said in back rooms. Even Julius Caesar in Shakespeare's famous play said, 'Et tu, Brute?' ('And you, Brutus?') as Brutus, his most trusted friend, plunged his dagger of betrayal into the side of his dying leader.

Had the disciples decided among themselves to 'push' Jesus a little? James and John would get their mother to test Jesus' plans, hoping his answer would give them some idea as to the imminence of the kingdom. Peter would bring a sword to the garden. (Why? Was there going to be a fight that he knew about?) Judas would bring in the opposition. Jesus would then have to make the final choice, and they must have been totally confident that he would.

They didn't want to betray Jesus; they simply wanted to start the fight that God would finish. They wanted 'their kingdom' to come, and all Jesus needed was their encouragement. After all, wasn't this why he had called them? Wasn't this why they had followed? Jesus had continually proclaimed, 'The kingdom of heaven is at hand'. This was their mission, and surely the mission was that important.

Peter, in a moment unlike any other in the Gospels, actually rose to the occasion and used the sword. But again, true to character, Jesus stepped in, protecting his enemies and healing their 'earless' servant.

The disciples had seen it time and time again: Jesus choosing to love an individual at the expense of the mission. The leper in Capernaum threatened to cast them all out of every city. The centurion put a price on their head as they became 'friends of Rome'. Their fellow disciple Matthew brought with him the scorn of the oppressed and poor. Jesus had insulted the Pharisees by breaking Levitical laws in order to heal a leper. He wagered everything every time. He put it all on the line, and always for one needy soul. The adulteress in the temple in Jerusalem. The woman in Sychar in Samaria. Zacchaeus in Jericho. All horribly fallen, flawed, irredeemable outcasts who were placed before the cause. What did that say about the disciples and their dreams? Didn't they deserve more? Surely there was something in it for them? Jesus couldn't ignore them after all this—could he?

Yet Jesus had even called Peter 'Satan'.

If we are looking for 'Antichrist' behaviour, surely it is this 'man-made kingdom' in the name of Jesus that puts self-centred ambition ahead of the kingdom of God.

Is this complicity too far-fetched? Perhaps. But when we pause to think about it, it may be that the established line of innocence is far more unbelievable, especially when we take into account all that we know about human nature. And remember, these men did not know what we know.

The stage was now set. The players had all been defined. On one side was humankind, represented by twelve disciples. After three years of seeing God first-hand they were none the wiser. They ended this part of their lives bickering, scheming and betraying.

On the other side was Jesus, alone. He had poured himself

out but it was still not enough. The multitudes had 'seen' God and they still wanted more—more miracles, more proof, more power. His friends were about to betray him. But Jesus replied to the intents of their hearts by washing

Jesus built a bridge from God's eternity, using his broken body as the girders and support beams.

their feet, a final gift that was an eternal depiction of God's eternal heart. His course was set and nothing would deviate him. Planet Earth was about to receive the final and decisive chapter of God's autobiography, the chapter in which every word ever written about God would find its foundation and fulfilment. Jesus was about to define God's nature on the cross, finally writing the 'Word made flesh' in all its fullness.

There was an absolute gulf between the actions of the disciples and the actions of Jesus. Jesus was about to finish his work by building a bridge that would forever traverse this chasm. He took bread and wine and started to build from the side of God's eternity, using his broken body as the girders and support beams. As the bridge was completed on the barren soil of earth, Jesus, the architect, engineer and builder, dedicated his masterpiece to his beloved but 'blind' friends and prepared a meal for them in their honour. He served the bread and wine, using these emblems to tell the story, hoping that people in each generation would finally understand.

All that was left was the final opening. The 'ribbon' must be cut.

Jesus went to the garden to pray.

Judas had already gone. Jesus' disciples were sleeping. He was alone. He had so little time. His mission called him to choose again, except the roles were now reversed. It was not his choice. Instead he had to surrender himself to humanity's choice. The disciples had seen Jesus choose man over mission time and time again. Now humanity had the upper hand, and it would decide to kill one man to protect its mission.

He cried out to his Father: 'Is there any other way?'

Suddenly the choice was so terrible. He could call down thousands of angels, but then he would have to deny all he had done up to this point. He would have to deny himself. He had come to save the world and nothing had deterred him. He had sought out the lost, preferring them over everything else, and had brought light into their darkness and love into their loveless world. Now the whole creation was about to wager itself on a bet concerning the identity of the Messiah. Humankind, lost in its need for kingdoms of power, was about to commit its greatest act of insurrection, and heaven itself would stagger at the absurdity. Jesus had come from eternity, and everything he had done, everything he had said, everything he was, was not enough. Now they were going to settle the matter once and for all. They were going to choose another Messiah, the Messiah of their hopes and dreams. Jesus had failed their expectations.

'Father, please remove this cup from me.'

The terror of this final act gripped him. He had washed their guilty feet, yet now even those who were so close had possibly conspired together.

Jesus was alone, about to be rendered obsolete as humanity's mission became more important than the man. And in this place, every retrenched worker, every deposed leader, every disgraced minister, every abandoned friend and rejected misfit, has a friend in Jesus.

'Father, please take this cup from me.'

Jesus had come to the core of humanity's hellish heart and he knew no one could come with him. He was so horribly abandoned and alone. He was at the end. Every weeping, tragic life that has cried, 'I can't go on', every desperate standing on the edge choosing life or death, now has a friend.

Somewhere, deep inside Jesus, the God that was all of him, yet all of man, found grace, forgiveness and mercy. Love burned, ached and longed for his brothers and sisters, and their deeds fell powerless at his feet. Love overcame. Jesus chose. He had all heaven's authority at his command and he chose humankind and laid down his life. Love triumphed. It overrode the authority of humanity. Jesus chose to die before he was sentenced by Pilate. Jesus, God's Son, humbled every power and authority, overturning it with the love of a servant heart.

Nothing could separate him from his love for them. Nothing they could do could dim this love—not one deed or act. His blood proved it. His death sealed it. His resurrection established it. Forever. The joy that was now set before him overwhelmed his fear and doubt, and he simply said: 'Not my will, but yours.'

> **God put his life ahead of ours by simply surrendering himself to our will.**

In a flash, in the farthest heaven, the angels looked on and saw God in a way that redefined all they had ever seen before. All the glory of all creation, all beauty, all majesty was humiliated by this act of love, so pure, deep, immeasurable and powerful.

If God can become any greater, he did so now, as his love exploded into an eternity of lost souls.

God put his life ahead of ours by simply surrendering himself to our will.

Extraordinary!

Jesus stood to his feet and went to wake his disciples. Come on, boys, the fight is just about to begin!

Before the night was out, it was horribly clear to the disciples that Jesus had not 'taken the bait'.

Peter tried to prevent his arrest but lost the fight when Jesus himself stepped in. Peter was broken by what he had done and what he could not undo. All his promises and words had meant nothing. He had completely failed in his cause, and his great enthusiasm deserted him.

He and another disciple (thought to be John) followed after Jesus, hoping somehow to rescue him. They sat by the fire in the courtyard of the high priest and waited. Only Peter's actions are mentioned: he could not find the courage even to admit that he was with Jesus. He turned away from his beloved master, swearing and cursing with the language of his past. He chose to save his own life. Peter, with Jesus and John looking on, denied his master three times.

Judas went to the chief priests and also tried to undo what he had done. Judas could not live with his betrayal. He pleaded Jesus' innocence, but the chief priests had all they needed. Judas was now expendable. His influence was gone. His master would die and he was the betrayer. He went and hanged himself.

The rest of the disciples ran for their lives, and for the first time in three years they were all alone with their guilt and grief.

And Jesus, the Son of the living God, was arrested and charged as Joseph's son from Nazareth. If his home town had known the events of this night, they would have felt vindicated.

13

Barabbas

Jerusalem was full of pilgrims. The nation had come together to celebrate the Passover. In between the prayers, the preparations and the celebrations, a strange event was taking place. In the middle of Jerusalem, the multitude had gathered before the Roman governor, Pontius Pilate. It was the custom for Pilate to release a prisoner at the Passover, so the crowd waited for this act of 'Roman grace'.

Three men faced the multitude that day: Pontius Pilate; Barabbas, who had committed murder in a rebellion, possibly being admired for his nationalistic zeal; and Jesus from Galilee.

We may well say that Jesus was unjustly accused, but it depends from which side you are looking. In the eyes of the Jewish ruling council and the high priest, Jesus was a blasphemer and a seditious prophet. His ministry threatened the power and integrity of Judaism. Many had proclaimed him the Messiah, and if they could get a confession from his lips, it would be enough to convince the Roman governor. This was the only way that the Jews could execute Jesus, because Rome had taken away their right to carry out capital punishment. If Jesus admitted he was the Messiah, he would indeed be a threat to the security of the Roman occupying force, and Pilate would have no choice. Jesus would be as guilty as Barabbas.

And Jesus *was* guilty of this crime. He *was* the Messiah!

But this wasn't why the Jews brought him to Pilate. The real crime he committed was that *he wasn't the Messiah they were looking for*. He wasn't what they expected, and therefore they rejected him. Now he must be rejected by all. That would settle the matter forever.

If you look back at the history of world leadership you will notice a pattern. Tomorrow's leaders carry a nation's hopes and expectations. Today's leaders are criticised for their failures. Yesterday's leaders are rejected by a disillusioned populace.

The same can be seen in our relationships as they falter and breakdown. Divorce lawyers have to mediate between couples who once 'couldn't bear to live apart' and now 'can't bear to be in the same room'. Love has a tragic way of becoming hate. What is once so full of hope ends up being so laden with blame.

Jesus had broken the dreams and dashed the hopes of those who 'were hoping that it was he who was going to redeem Israel'. Pilate presented to the multitude in Jerusalem the opportunity to turn their hope into hate.

> But Pilate answered them, saying, 'Do you want me to release to you the King of the Jews?' But the chief priests stirred up the crowd, so that he should rather release Barabbas to them.

We have grown up with this story. Perhaps you have seen it portrayed in videos and movies. We have probably come to some strong conclusions.

What would *you* have said on that fateful day? Would you have yelled 'Jesus' or 'Barabbas'?

But what would *you* have said on that fateful day in Jerusalem? Would you have yelled 'Jesus' or 'Barabbas'?

Let me challenge you. You are standing there in the crowd. Pilate is saying, 'Do you want this Jesus to be released to you, this King of the Jews? Or do you want the zealot, Barabbas, a political martyr?' You have to make your choice.

You are a Jew. You love the Lord God with all your heart and mind and strength. You love the law and the prophets. You are waiting for the Messiah. Your life here in Jerusalem revolves around the sacrifices and offerings at the temple. You have a great respect for all those who work in the Lord's name. The high priest, the chief priests, the Pharisees and the scribes are well known to you. You trust them, you honour them, you believe them.

Jesus, however, you don't know so well. It is said that he could be the Messiah. You have heard the rumours. It seems like the whole of Galilee has been caught up in the controversy concerning his work. At the beginning of the week there was a strange procession as these Galileans, arriving en masse for the Passover, tore palm fronds from the trees lining the road and sang his praises. Where are they now?

You see the priests walking through the crowd and they are speaking against Jesus. That is a pretty good indication as to his authenticity. The priests are not fools.

But what of the claims of Jesus and his followers? You have heard about the miracles, the healings, the resurrections. Surely God must be with this man, for nothing like this has happened for generations. Rumour has it that Jesus took some bread and fish and fed thousands of men, women and children, with plenty left over. This sounds like manna in the wilderness of Galilee.

You look at the man standing next to Pilate's judgment seat. He looks at peace, even settled and confident. He certainly does not carry the wild look of a demon-possessed prophet with a dangerous cult following. You have seen such men and their crazed followers many times before, and they always disappear as quickly as they appear.

Standing there in the crowd, looking around, you reason with yourself. If he isn't guilty of the charges they are bringing against him—and Pilate seems very dubious about them—then he should be released. But if he isn't guilty, then it follows he must be innocent. And if he is innocent, then perhaps he is telling the truth and he *is* the One. The Messiah!

You look at him again. *Is* this the Messiah? Has he come? Your heart skips a beat.

You think on. If he is the Messiah then everything must change. The high priest, the chief priests, all the Pharisees, the Jewish ruling council, all who have been ordained of God, every man is wrong. In fact, they are more than wrong; they are guilty. They are as guilty as this Jesus is innocent.

You avert your eyes as a priest walks by. Suddenly this is not a simple choice about who is released and who is crucified. This is the most important issue, and for a minute you feel overwhelmingly alone in your decision. Just you and God. Just your heart and this man, Jesus.

Suddenly you are shaken out of your thoughts as one of the chief priests walks up to you. You can't make this decision by yourself, so you summon your courage and ask him, 'What has this man done that is so wrong?'

The chief priest hears the question and stifles his anger. He is determined to keep his dignity intact through all of this. How he wishes they could have settled it themselves, behind the closed door of their council. But the Romans have made a public spectacle of this man. They have dared to call him 'King of the Jews'. He will not dignify this with his anger. The case is clear. It simply needs to be explained.

He answers: 'Would you expect the Messiah to come from Galilee? Wouldn't God send him to Jerusalem? This Jesus was thrown out of his home town in very suspicious circumstances. That town, Nazareth, a tiny village in the back hills of Galilee, has endured the shame of this man since his conception. He spurned the good will of his family and friends. He turned his back on their protection and their loyalty to his father's good name. Nazareth will have nothing to do with him. His brothers don't believe. Does this sound like the Messiah to you?

'His first "miracle", if you can call it that, was a simple trick with cheap wine that he and his disciples had taken to a wedding, hidden in water jars. This wine was given to some guests after they had demolished the cellar. If he were the Messiah, wouldn't he have sent them home with a good lesson from the law? But no: the bride and groom actually sold the dregs and made a small profit! Would the Messiah become a wine merchant?

'And listen to what he did in Capernaum. He told a man that his sins were forgiven. Yes, the Messiah could do that—but after breaking the law and touching a leper? He was unclean at the time. Would the Messiah ever allow himself to be unclean? Would the Messiah ever break the law?

'Then he went to a tax collector's booth and made this outcast a disciple. No training, no college, nothing. And then he and his new disciples—fishermen, if you please—went to a party in this tax collector's house. And it gets worse, my friend. Would the Messiah even talk to a centurion? Jesus healed one centurion's accursed servant and then pronounced that this horrid soldier had more faith than all of Israel! His friends are prostitutes, Samaritans, sinners, publicans.

'If you are looking for any more proof, let me tell you what his disciples think of him. Do you see them anywhere. How do you think this Jesus was arrested? One of his closest friends came to us. When we arrived, his other disciples were obviously full of too much food and wine. There was a small struggle, but the helpers of this "Messiah" had no fight in them at all. Says something about their doubts, doesn't it? We took this Jesus, and one of his friends followed us. When he was challenged, he swore so loudly that even the soldiers blushed. Do you need any more proof?

'To be sure, God gives you the right to choose this man as your Messiah. But if you do, know that you choose against the will and wisdom of the entire Jewish council, right up to the high priest himself. In fact, you do more than choose in spite of us. By choosing Jesus you reject us. If he is innocent, then you must declare us guilty. And all that you hold dear is wrong.'

The chief priest moves on, encouraged by his defence. It is so obvious. Why hadn't Capernaum dealt with it three years ago?

You are left in the crowd and you have to make your decision.

Jesus or Barabbas?

This question is not answered in a crowd two thousand years ago. It is answered every day that our expectations concerning God contradict who he really is. When we define God in such a way that others are humiliated and judged and rejected, lines are drawn and absolutes proclaimed and defended, we may as well simply yell 'Barabbas!'

When I defend 'my Jesus' and judge 'your Jesus', I am crying out 'Barabbas!'

When we choose our systems, our administrations, our moralities, our desires, our powers and authorities, discriminating against and judging those who do not agree with us, we are yelling 'Barabbas!'

> **When we define God in such a way that others are judged and rejected, we may as well simply yell 'Barabbas!'**

Be honest. If Jesus came to the 21st century, if he did the same things in our culture as he did in Galilee and Judea, what would you say—especially if every church leader had such doubts that they turned him over to the police?

Let's sit in our pews and hold the bread and the wine and ask ourselves the question. What would we have said? Whose name is continually in our judgmental hearts and on our judgmental lips?

Join me, before I eat the bread and drink the cup. Before we thank God for his unmerited grace, mercy and forgiveness, let us come to the awful realisation of what he has forgiven us for doing.

We cannot taste grace until we admit we have been saying the name 'Barabbas'.

We cannot understand the fullness of his love until we admit that we have been a Peter, a James, a John and a Judas.

In Jerusalem that day were two mothers, both grieving for their sons. Overwhelmed by fear and hopelessness, their only hope was in God's mercy. So, kneeling in different rooms in different parts of this Holy City, they prayed that God would be merciful.

God in heaven heard their prayers and answered them with the greatest revelation of the divine nature.

One mother, Mary, watched as her son died at the hands of his brothers and sisters. The other mother welcomed her son home, saying, with grateful tears in her eyes, 'Barabbas! God has answered our prayers!'

Another man more important than the mission. Jesus died on Barabbas's cross . . . our cross.

14

The Beach

Failure.

God comes to our failure, because of our failure, the absolute victim of our failure. Yes, we wish it was otherwise, but the awful truth is that we have failed. We want to be right, we want to be approved, we want to be blessed and we are desperate for God to fulfil our needs. Our hurting and wounded souls yearn for vindication, for our enemies to be punished and our sins understood. We want a God who takes our side and fights our fight, making our pain, humiliation and victimisation worth enduring. We want to win and we want 'the others' to lose.

We feel deep destructive desires. A child is murdered—we want judgment. A nation is plundered—we want judgment. We are wronged, misunderstood and abused—we want judgment. We want a God who will agree with our hatred and carry out our threats.

God could take sides. He could feel a deep revulsion against the guilty perpetrators who judge the innocent. He could demand justice. But what if he did? What if God really took sides? Whose side would he take? What would we ask him to do? Who is on our list?

Who is on God's list?

Are you able to be honest here? Can you uncover your wounded heart, visiting again the anger and the helplessness? Can you again hear your thoughts, listening to your own vengeful words? Can you then find, within your dark murderous heart, the desire to pray judgment on those who have hurt you and your loved ones?

Join with me in a deep, heart-felt prayer to God, a prayer that needs God himself to intervene and take sides. I have prayed this prayer so many times. I have felt the frustration, the anger, the depression, the helplessness and the hopelessness, and I have prayed:

'Oh God do something!'

Then I look at the cross and realise that God has answered my cry, but not the way I desired. Whose side did God take? When all his children could not bear to believe in the God of Jesus Christ, choosing instead to release a criminal and place Jesus on this criminal's cross, whose side did God take?

Did he demand justice? Did he demand vindication? Did he swoop down from heaven and say, 'Enough is enough'?

Humankind yelled 'Barabbas!' and Jesus remained silent. He did not defend himself. He did not bring a case that would have proved his innocence and Barabbas's guilt. No, he accepted our choice and died on Barabbas's cross.

Barabbas was as guilty as Jesus was innocent.

We chose Barabbas's side and put Jesus alone on the other. All of humankind against one man. All of humankind against God.

We made our choice and, in the eyes of God, we became as guilty as Barabbas. Then we received Barabbas's remission because Jesus died on our cross.

In fact, I believe it goes further. As we look at these final days of Jesus' life on earth, we see ourselves in James and John, plotting our places of power and authority in the kingdom. We see ourselves in Peter, misunderstanding Jesus, still trying to earn favour, unable to simply accept and receive. When Jesus' mission ends in failure, we run away with the disciples. If we have the courage and honesty, we see ourselves in Judas, enthroning our desires and needs until we end up denying the reality of God that Jesus came to reveal. Our interpretations and expectations become our reality and we betray Jesus.

How can we ask him to take sides when it is so eternally apparent that he has already?

'Test me, try me, maim me, kill me. See if it will make any difference to my love for you.'

If I ask God to judge, then I had better be first in line.

Failure. It is our failure that now reveals the glory of God—the immensity of God's forgiveness, mercy, grace and love. This glory has to be applied to the very worst of our human heart, the place where our seared consciences demand that God allow us the right to 'judge' while we remain 'beyond judgment'. We ask him to join our judgment. We even say that he will carry it out for us! God's immense love is clearly seen rising above the cancer of our vain, shallow, broken self-righteousness. The glory of God is proclaimed in his steadfast refusal to change his character, no matter what the provocation. God declares that his love will never be subject to our actions.

'*Test me, try me, maim me, kill me. See if it will make any difference to my love for you.*'

This glory is God's response to us—refusing to retreat from his mission of love in spite of all we do, both to him and to each other. This can only be seen from the viewpoint of failure and absolute unworthiness. In the midst of the doom of eternal wrath, in the shadow of death, God's comfort, God's love, God's grace is totally unexpected, totally unmerited, totally undeserved and totally glorious.

Recently, the 'Today Show' on Australian early morning television has been following a story from Vancouver, Canada. It concerns a group of policemen who, frustrated by every generation repeating the excesses of the past, set about producing a documentary about heroin addicts living on the streets. Initially it was meant to be a stark warning to the next generation; their mandate was not to help the addicts but simply record the degradation of their lives. To do this, however, the policemen had to follow these wretched men and woman around, interview them, record their day-to-day existence on video. Relationships started to form as the addicts began to feel safer with a camera than they were with handcuffs. Before long, the 'headline' had a life, a 'story'.

The addicts had names! So did the policemen!

For the first time in a long time these addicts had friends—and of all people, it was with their former enemies. Slowly, one by one, they entered rehabilitation. Why? Because at last they were loved in the midst of their failure.

Their enemy joined them. Their enemy loved them. And in the words of one of the officers, 'compassion started to flow'.

Failure. Can you see it? From God's perspective we are all marked with the word 'failure'. We are all his enemies. God answers us on the cross of our failure. He is our ultimate victim as we judge him for not transforming himself into the image of our wisdom and judgments. We want him to be on 'our side' so that we can continue to build structures that ennoble us at the expense of others. We misrepresent him and then demand that others believe the same. When he 'fails' us we refute him, defending our works and denying his.

In Australia we appear to be more concerned with pointing out the 'sin' of addiction rather than saving the 'life' of the addict. Tell me, who is more sinful at the cross—the addict we judge or us, the judges? Then tell me who is less aware of their sin? Where would we be if Jesus took the same approach to us?

And yet we still manage to find in ourselves and our 'faith' the misplaced confidence to judge.

The cross demands of us all, addicts and judges alike, that we see our sinfulness as it really is. Only then can we admit that we are all unworthy—unworthy of grace, unworthy to judge. Only then can we make the vulnerable journey to become responsible for our own actions as we accept their consequences. The addict becomes responsible for the pain he has inflicted on himself, his family and his friends. The judges become responsible for the grace that they have received and set about healing those they have wounded. The addict discovers the heart of God and is forever grateful, for he has nothing to lose and everything to gain. The judge has to leave behind his blatant self-righteousness before he can ever 'see' the grace that he lives in. Until this happens, he will continue to close the doors to those whose only hope lies on 'the other side'. Only the guilty can truly 'see' the beauty of grace.

The Vancouver Police Department is modelling Christ to us. Some addicts will rehabilitate. Some will not. But all the addicts that come into contact with these officers will know love and compassion. Those who die (and they die daily) will not die alone. Surely one life is worth the effort. This will not stop heroin addiction, but it may preserve a life.

Yes, we feel the need to make a stand against what is wrong. But again, look at the cross. What did Jesus say about Barabbas's wrongs? As always, the answer was more in what he did than what he said. Jesus' answer to Barabbas's sin was the silent action of grace. I wonder what Barabbas thought when Jesus was resurrected and he heard the news that this carpenter from Nazareth was the Messiah? What images ran through Barabbas's mind whenever he heard the message that Jesus died in his place?

We often have so much to say about sin and so little to do about it. But Jesus always had a lot less to say and more to do.

I remember my first trip to Nairobi. My wife, Victoria, and I were the guests of World Vision. We were driven from the airport to our hotel. On the way we were shown the sights of the city. A colonial past jostled with the buildings of a free nation struggling to establish itself. I do not remember the buildings, which is strange because I love architecture. I can only remember the faces of the families living in the streets. I can only remember the images of the children begging in the busy intersections. I can only remember the hungry, innocent smiles in the ghettos, amidst the squalor and fear. My songs did not mean a bean to these people. My messages were meaningless until they could see the love and compassion of Christ standing unconditionally with them. Only the living can bring life and love. Words are meaningless until they become flesh. Jesus gave life to Barabbas long before Barabbas ever knew the truth. I don't have any other model to use, so my worship must be modelled on his life as my lyrics become flesh and blood.

Jesus gave life to Barabbas long before Barabbas ever knew the truth.

As we look from our guilty hearts to the empty cross of Barabbas and then to the face of Jesus, we must surely feel moved by a deep personal sense of overwhelming relief and gratitude. In the light of this we cannot remain removed, and we cannot descend to judgment. We must rise with Jesus to life, to live indebted to the grace that we have been given, to give unconditionally as we have received unconditionally, to love passionately as we are loved passionately.

This is the way of the cross, and it is glorified whenever failure is overwhelmed by the life of God in us.

Imagine the scenes in Jerusalem as one by one the disciples heard the news that Jesus had risen. What went through their minds? What did Peter think? What did John and James think? When Jesus finally appeared to them, he went to Thomas and presented his wounds, and asked his hopelessly disappointed disciple to 'do whatever he needed to do' to believe. On the cross Jesus had already done all that he could possibly do to show us himself. All he could offer to Thomas were his broken hands, wounded feet and gashed side. 'Whatever it takes, Thomas, do not leave here unbelieving.'

Jesus offered his brokenness as an ointment, pleading with Thomas to see his glory through Thomas's failure.

Can we live the life of 'whatever it takes'? Will we bare our wounds, as Jesus did, so that others can see?

Jesus was resurrected in Jerusalem. I have visited what is believed to be the 'Garden Tomb', just outside the walls of the Old City. There you will find a cave with a large round stone that has been 'rolled away' from its small entrance. This tomb is in a restored garden from Jesus' time. It is a tranquil place, surrounded by a stone wall. It was discovered late in the nineteenth century lying a hundred or so metres away from a rocky cliff that is in the unmistakable shape of a skull.

We celebrated communion late one afternoon in this garden and reflected on the identity of God as he walked free from death, our death. This return from the grave is the final evidence of God's life revealed to us in Jesus. This life lived among us, cried with us, hurt with us, suffered with us, all so it could finally suffer at our hands. This life knew such pain and still chose 'not my will but yours'—a will that finds its focus and fulfilment in us, in our treachery, faithlessness and failure. This life, having accepted the hard road, then suffered more so it could cry with us, 'I am God-forsaken'—then rise ahead of us to prove that we can never be forsaken by God. This life declares we are adopted by God.

All this we celebrated with a small cup and a tiny fragment of bread. Bread and wine that proves the worst of humankind. Bread and wine that was once mutilated flesh and pools of blood. We acknowledged our failure as we all quietly and simply confessed that we had spoken the name 'Barabbas'. We then looked at the bread and wine in our hands to realise what this, the 'worst' of us, said about God. God turns mutilation into celebration. We celebrated this communion as a confession that God had turned the worst of us into the best of himself. We then walked out of the garden to follow the footsteps of Jesus.

The footsteps of Jesus led him back to Galilee. Why? Surely Jerusalem was the place where the news of the resurrection would have its greatest effect. It was only days since the Passover and the Holy City was still full of pilgrims. Surely Jesus and his disciples could have preached on every street corner and a revival would have broken out?

Jesus, however, chose to go to Galilee. He told his disciples to go home and he would meet them there. What emotions were running through their hearts? What questions were running through their minds?

One thing is for sure, the expectations of the journey to Jerusalem had been overwhelmed by the events of their last week with Jesus. Underneath the relief and joy of his resurrection was the shame and guilt of their part in his crucifixion. Could it be that this resurrection proved the very things that we, two thousand years later, confessed at the 'Garden Tomb'— things that left these poor disciples feeling humiliated by all they had thought, said and done? Now that it was so very clear who Jesus was, they felt utterly disqualified from doing anything more in his name.

Yes, Jesus had triumphed over death. But they had failed miserably. Now they were going home, alone.

What awaited them in Galilee? What were they going to say about their last meal together? How was Peter ever going to explain his actions around the courtyard fire? What were they going to say about Judas? Above all these questions was the one that filled them with the most apprehension: what was *Jesus* going to say to *them*? He was now truly revealed as the Messiah, the Son of the living God. Why did he tell them to go home? What was he going to do with them in Galilee that he couldn't do in Jerusalem?

Again Jesus seemed to have gone in an unexpected direction, confounding his disciples in the process.

How would you feel? I would be sick in the stomach with the

awful dread of impending judgment. My sin would demand that I prepare myself for whatever consequences were rightly coming my way. No matter how glorious the resurrection, I would be chained to the shame of my own horrid actions.

They walked through Jericho, past Zacchaeus's tree. They walked through the wilderness where John the Baptist had lived and ministered. They crossed the Jordan where Andrew and Peter had first met Jesus. Then they came again to Capernaum by the Sea of Galilee. They returned broken, defeated and guilty to their families and friends.

What did they say when everyone asked, 'What happened to Jesus?' What did Peter say to his wife and mother-in-law when he came home to his house, his table and his bed?

What was ahead of them? What was left for them to do? The dream had died. They had seen to it themselves. Their memories taunted them. His words rang in their ears and they remembered him—all he did, all he said and all he was.

They had failed him. They had failed God.

How could they have been so horribly wrong?

It was over. It had finished.

Peter finally said, 'I am going fishing.' Did he really mean, 'I am going back to fishing'? 'I will take out the old boat, open the old accounts, go back to my old profession and start again.' What else can a failed disciple do?

Do you know this failure? I do. Thousands upon thousands over the centuries do.

Peter was not alone. Thomas, Nathaniel, James, John and two others felt the same, and together they set out in Peter's boat to fish for their living.

Failure.

Just as Jesus left eternity to reveal his love for the failed, he now left the place of greatest influence, the place where he could have preached from the temple, humiliating every member of the Jewish ruling council, the chief priests and the high priest, shaming every man, woman and child that had dared to yell 'Barabbas!' Jesus could have established his kingdom there and then on the throne of David, but he didn't. He left Jerusalem because he had to find his desperately broken and forlorn friends. He followed them.

The footsteps of Jesus follow the failed and the broken.

He returned to where it all began. Jesus came again to Capernaum, the home of Peter, James and John, and again he came alone. No great angelic procession. No thunderous acclamation from the heavens. He arrived around dawn one morning and stood on the shore of the Sea of Galilee, looking for his friends. Perhaps in the early light he walked up and down the beach, cupping one hand over his eyes as he searched the horizon through the early morning glare. He looked for a boat among many boats. All the fishermen of Galilee would have been out that morning, but only one boat carried such disappointment. Only one boat carried the failure that was the key to seeing his glory. One boat. Six broken men, starting life all over again.

Six headlines. Six stories. The gospel was about to be revealed.

Good news for failures!

What had been the conversation that night on the lake as these former disciples relearnt their old skills, blistering their hands on the oars, ropes and nets? What did they say as their hopelessness turned into despair as they now failed even at fishing? They caught nothing. Did they feel absolutely Godforsaken?

Jesus walked along the beach and could not see his friends. What did he do? Did he summon the wind and waves to drive these foolish men out of their 'backsliding'? Did he step onto the water to overwhelm them with his deity? Did his voice thunder from the skies? What did God do with their failure?

Jesus started to collect driftwood. He obtained some fish and bread. He lit a small fire and, blowing on the coals, began to cook. Jesus had come, thinking purely about their welfare, to meet their needs.

He was making breakfast for his hungry friends.

Suddenly he looked up from his cooking and saw the boat. I have walked many beaches dotted with failed fishermen and have said the same simple greeting, 'Caught anything?' Now the answer to Jesus' inquiry drifted forlornly across the water: 'No.'

'Then cast the net on the right side of the boat, and you will find some.'

Jesus challenged them to start again, but differently. Put the net out the other side. It is a new day. Try again, but this time, try differently.

When we have failed, we know we cannot go back, for we have already proved to ourselves and to others that we cannot make the grade. We cannot maintain the discipline or complete the work. When we have failed, we have been disqualified by the very methods that we had hoped would affirm us.

But Jesus says to us all, 'Come on, throw the net out the other side. Don't give up. Failure is not the end. It's just another beginning. Don't look at what you've done, look at what I'm doing.'

The disciples' nets filled with fish and for an instant they felt the flush of success. Perhaps they looked at each other and said; 'It's okay, we can do this. Life will go on. We can still fish. We'll make it, boys!' Then something clicked in Peter and he remembered: 'This is how it all began.' He looked from the false hope of a net full of fish, the affirmation of his work, to the only one who could make sense of his failure, the only one who could answer the desperate cry of his heart, the only one who could bring back his peace, hope and joy.

Peter looked, and he saw the same familiar shape that stood on the shore three long, failed years ago. He remembered the hope and the promise. It seemed like a miracle, as if Jesus has turned back time and was offering the same wonderful love all over again.

'It is the Lord!'

When your footsteps lead you back down the path of humiliation and disgrace, when you leave behind the great opportunities, when you are disgraced and fallen, you are followed. Jesus leaves the 'mission' and follows the 'man'. He searches for you, waits for you, loves you and cares for you. In his heart is a simple concern: your welfare. The hot coals, the bread and the fish prove it.

> **When your footsteps lead down the path of disgrace, you are followed. Jesus searches for you.**

Peter jumped into the water and swam to Jesus.

What could Jesus have said? Perhaps: 'Cock-a-doodle-doo, Pete!' Or: 'Remember the last fire we stood around?' Instead Jesus simply looked at Simon Peter, a fisherman from Galilee, an ordinary man with a litany of guilt stacked up against him. Jesus looked into the eyes that had turned away, into the heart that was guilty of the worst, and he said:

'Peter, do you love me?'

Three times. Each time answering Peter's tragic denial. Three times Jesus turned betrayal into acceptance. The end becomes the beginning.

'Peter, look at my eyes. Tell me if you see any rejection, any disappointment. Do you now understand my love? You never earned it, you never deserved it, and you never broke it. Can you now accept this and pass it on? Feed my lambs, Peter. Feed my lambs with *this* love.'

I have stood on that beach. I have looked out over the Sea of Galilee. I have walked up and down its shoreline, strewn with pebbles. And I have imagined the fire and the fish. However, I do not need to go to Israel to stand in this place, for its only significance is in the fact that Jesus came here to find his friends and to give them hope and encourage them to start again.

It may take us a lifetime of fishing to realise that there is a figure waiting on *our* shoreline, waiting for *us* to recognise who he really is. Waiting for us to turn from 'earning' to 'accepting'. We can choose to look away, humiliated by our inadequacy; we can refuse him his identity, preferring to retreat into our own concepts of how God should deal with us; we can bury our hope in activity. But that will never change who he is, what he has done and what he expects of us.

Jesus wants all of us who have failed to lift our head, open our eyes and smell the enticing aroma of baked bread and BBQ fish.

Only God could have come up with such a plan. When you recognise this aroma of salvation, every failed life is accompanied by a solitary figure baking fish on a small campfire. He looks up at you and simply asks:

'Will you join me?'

Postscript

An old man sat at a table and remembered. His mind wandered back to Galilee. So many times he had shaken his head in awe as the significance of these memories continued to challenge his beliefs and his worship.

Peter was entirely different from the man who once stood on the mountain with Moses, Elijah and Jesus. He thought of his words that day as Jesus was transfigured before him. Love overwhelmed him as the simple beauty of God's patient grace was again so evident in his precious master's eyes.

Peter remembered and again smelled the bread and fish. Every memory finished with this aroma of hope.

There were no words, no deeds, no songs, nothing that could do justice to what he now knew of Jesus. He had seen Jesus through the eyes of betrayal.

Every day now was a gift.

He looked at the parchment and pen lying on the table and read again the start of his letter. He wished it could say more, but he knew it couldn't. The words remained on the paper. The life behind them, around them and in them remained in his heart.

He prayed, 'Jesus, my Lord, my friend, please make these words into flesh.'

Peter, an apostle of Jesus Christ . . .
Blessed be the God and Father of our Lord Jesus Christ, who according to His abundant mercy has begotten us again to a living hope through the resurrection of Jesus Christ from the dead, to an inheritance incorruptible and undefiled and that does not fade away, reserved in heaven for you, who are kept by the power of God through faith for salvation ready to be revealed in the last time.
In this you greatly rejoice, though now for a little while, if need be, you have been grieved by various trials, that the genuineness of your faith, being much more precious than gold that perishes, though it is tested by fire, may be found to praise, honour and glory at the revelation of Jesus Christ, whom having not seen you love.
Though now you do not see Him, yet believing, you rejoice with joy inexpressible and full of glory, receiving the end of your faith—the salvation of your souls.

References

Chapter 1: Interpretations and Expectations
Philip Yancey, *What's So Amazing About Grace?* Grand Rapids: Zondervan, 1997, p. 70.

Chapter 2: The Grace of His Coming
Isaiah 9:6–7
Luke 23:34

Chapter 3: The Stage Is Set
Isaiah 64:1–3
Psalm 19:1
Psalm 23:5

Chapter 4: Nazareth
Isaiah 53:1–3 (modified)
Luke 2:41–52: Jesus visits the temple as a boy.
Luke 2:52
Luke 4:16–30: Jesus is rejected at Nazareth.

Chapter 5: Arise, Shine
Isaiah 60:1–3
Isaiah 53:4; 57:15

Chapter 6: Cana
Isaiah 54:1, 4–5; 55:1–3
Matthew 3:15–17
John 1:29–51: Jesus is baptised and calls the brothers, Andrew and Simon (Peter).
John 2:1–12: The first miracle at Cana.

Chapter 7: Capernaum
Isaiah 61:1–3
Matthew 4:13–22; Mark 1:14–20; Luke 5:1–11: Jesus calls the disciples by the Sea of Galilee.
John 1:43–46: Philip and Nathanael
Matthew 4:23–25
Mark 1:33–34
Matthew 9:1–13; Mark 2:1–17; Luke 5:17–39: Jesus heals the paralytic and calls Matthew the tax–collector. Note: Matthew's given name was Levi. His apostolic name was Matthew, meaning 'gift of God' (margin note for Mark 2:14–15, *Spirit-Filled Life Bible*).
Comment on 'tax collectors and sinners' taken from the *Spirit-Filled Life Bible*, Nashville: Thomas Nelson, 1991.

Chapter 8: Outcasts
Matthew 8:1–13: Jesus heals the leper and the centurion's servant.
John 15:13

Chapter 9: John the Baptist
Isaiah 40:3
Malachi 4:5–6; Luke 1:17, 76
Matthew 3:1–17; Mark 1:1–11; Luke 3:1–22; John 1:19–34: John the Baptist's ministry begins and Jesus is baptised at the Jordan River.

Matthew 11:2–19; Luke 7:18–35: John the Baptist questions Jesus' identity.
John 3:22–36: John the Baptist defends Jesus.

Chapter 10: Peter
Matthew 16:15
Matthew 17:1–13: The Transfiguration.
Mark 9:33
Matthew 16:13–20: Peter's 'revelation'.
Matthew 16:21–23: Peter's 'agenda'.

Chapter 11: Rich, Young and Upwardly Mobile
Matthew 19:16–26; Mark 10:17–27; Luke 18:18–27: The rich young ruler.
Matthew 5:3

Chapter 12: The Garden
Matthew 20:20–23: James and John's mother makes a request.
John 13:1–20: Jesus washes the disciples' feet.
Matthew 26:26–29; Mark 14:22–25; Luke 22:17–20: Jesus breaks bread and shares the cup.
Matthew 26:36–75; Mark 14:32–72; Luke 22:39–62; John 18:1–18: The tragic finale in the garden.

Chapter 13: Barabbas
Luke 24:21
Mark 15:6–15: Barabbas.

Chapter 14: The Beach
John 21:1–25: The beach.

Postscript
1 Peter 1:1–9